Affirmative Action
on Trial

LANDMARK LAW CASES

&

AMERICAN SOCIETY

Peter Charles Hoffer

N. E. H. Hull

Series Editors

MELVIN I. UROFSKY

Affirmative Action on Trial

Sex Discrimination in *Johnson v. Santa Clara*

UNIVERSITY PRESS OF KANSAS

Published by the University Press of Kansas (Lawrence, Kansas 66049), which was
organized by the Kansas Board of Regents and is operated and funded by Emporia
State University, Fort Hays State University, Kansas State University, Pittsburg State
University, the University of Kansas, and Wichita State University

Library of Congress Cataloging-in-Publication Data
Urofsky, Melvin I.
Affirmative action on trial : sex discrimination in Johnson v.
Santa Clara / Melvin I. Urofsky.
p.   cm.
Includes bibliographical references and index.
ISBN 0-7006-0829-x (alk. paper). —
ISBN 0-7006-0830-3 (pbk. : alk. paper)
1. Johnson, Paul, 1925–   — Trials, litigation, etc.   2. Santa
Clara County Transportation Agency — Trials, ligitation etc.
3. Reverse discrimination in employment — Law and legislation — United
States.   4. Reverse discrimination in employment — California — Santa
Clara County.   I. Title.
KF228.J64U758   1997
342.73'087 — dc21   96-39511

British Library Cataloguing in Publication Data is available.

Printed in the United States of America
10 9 8 7 6 5 4 3 2

The paper used in this publication meets the minimum requirements of the American
National Standard for Permanence of Paper for Printed Library Materials
Z39.48-1984.

For

SHIRLEY PASSOW AND THE LATE A. HARRY PASSOW

two very special people

CONTENTS

As Melvin Urofsky demonstrates in this humane and thoughtful account of one affirmative action case, the losers in such suits are often without blame. From the end of the nineteenth century through the first half of the twentieth, private law in America has implicated conceptions of blameworthiness. It was the neglectful manufacturer, the intentional inflicter of harm, and the willful breaker of a contract who had to pay for their misdeeds. A revolution in private law after World War II changed some of these conceptions, at least in the law courts. The imposition of what is called "strict liability" for harms — you do it, you pay — transformed rules of private liability.

But what about public harms inflicted over the course of decades by one group of people, whose leaders were often clothed with the immunity of public office, upon another group of people? Could the concept of strict accountability be applied to the children of the first group? Did they owe some duty to repair the lives of the children of the second group? What role had history — a long history of actual harms imposed upon a minority simply because they were a minority — played in the decisions of courts? Or were the only histories that mattered those of the individuals who came before the court as plaintiff and defendant?

Whatever the justice of these questions, the political ramifications were clear. Throughout the 1970s, affirmative action programs in the forms of quotas, preferences, and set-asides based on race, gender, and other categories spelled out in federal law proliferated. Hiring and promotion in public services, public education, and private businesses that depended on state and federal contracts deployed affirmative action programs of one kind or another. The U.S. Supreme Court ruled out those programs that relied solely upon such criteria as race but did permit purely statistical evidence of past discrimination to support claims for preferential treatment. One law professor, writing in 1980, judged, "It is all over but the shouting." Affirmative action was an established part of American public law.

The problem was that the losers in affirmative action were not always the perpetrators of the original harm. They did not set out to deny fair treatment to people of color, women, or any other members of the "suspect categories" defined by law. What was their remedy? Moreover, most affirmative action programs were meant to last a finite period of time — until the favored minority could boost itself up to equal footing with the majority in the pool of applicants. Of course, such metaphors of level playing fields and starting lines are as much wishful thinking as accurate depiction, but law always works by analogy. Could courts determine in real time, not in the timeless world of constitutional doctrine, when such equality had been achieved?

The question that courts faced was thus not one of the constitutionality of affirmative action pure and simple but one of the social and economic realities in which the affirmative action programs were imbedded. Since *Santa Clara* was decided, federal appeals courts in a number of the circuits have ruled definitively against existing affirmative action programs. In states as divergent as California and Mississippi, governors and legislatures have taken steps against further implementation of affirmative action. The attorney general of the state of Georgia has advised the regents of the University of Georgia that their affirmative action plans may be unconstitutional. No subject of study in our legal history is more vital now than Professor Urofsky's, and few make more compelling reading.

There is an old story of two feuding peasants in a small eastern European village who finally appealed to the rabbi to resolve their dispute. The first peasant went in and with great emotion told the rabbi his side of the story. The rabbi listened carefully and then said, "You are right!"

Then the second peasant went in and with equal fervor and conviction presented his case. The rabbi considered for a moment, looked very thoughtful, and then said, "My son, you are right!"

The rabbi's wife, who had been sitting quietly in the corner while both men made their appeal, could hardly restrain herself until the second peasant left the room. "What have you done?" she cried. "You told both of them they were right! How could you do that?"

The rabbi scratched his head for a second and then turned to his wife. "And you, my dear," he said, "you are also right!"

————

As one looks at the social and legal aspects of affirmative action in general and of the *Johnson* case in particular, one often feels like this poor rabbi, wanting to shout out, "You are both right!" Except for extremists, most people recognize that affirmative action and the social and economic conditions that are behind it are very complex and not amenable to simple or easy answers. It is not a question of good versus evil, an obviously correct policy as opposed to one obviously wrong, and certainly not a story of good guys and bad guys. The story that follows, stories actually, of Paul Johnson and Diane Joyce, of Steve Woodside and Connie Brooks, of Michael Baratz and Kristy Sermersheim, of William Brennan and Antonin Scalia, are not stories of heroes and villains.

In spring 1987, shortly after the Court handed down its decision in the *Johnson* case, I told a friend that I thought it would make a good case study. *Johnson* not only involved a difficult question of law and an even harder problem in social policy, but here one could also see how great issues and cases affected common people, men and women who go to work every day, and whose lives, whether they want it or not, are affected by policies over which they have little control.

Santa Clara County saw that it had no women in a skilled-craft category in its Transportation Agency; it instituted an affirmative action plan to remedy what it recognized as a problem and also to foreclose potential lawsuits. Diane Joyce and Paul Johnson both applied for a particular skilled job, that of road dispatcher. Joyce believed she qualified and would be frozen out by the old-boy network in the agency, so she appealed to the affirmative action officer and eventually got the job. Johnson thought he had earned the position and had been discriminated against. She did not see herself as a feminist heroine; she was a widow who needed to earn more money for her family. He did not see himself as a David battling the bureaucratic Goliaths but as a person who had had something stolen from him that he wanted back. So he did what many Americans do every day of the year — they appeal to the law for redress. Sometimes it works for them, and sometimes not.

Interestingly, when I interviewed Paul Johnson and Diane Joyce, both of them said they wanted fairness, they wanted equal opportunity, they wanted to be judged on their own merits. They came at these ideals from different angles, but in an ideal world one would not find the two of them that far apart. They are very much old-fashioned Americans who believe fervently in their country and in its promise of equality for all under the law.

Ultimately it was their human stories, and not the broader issue of affirmative action, that drew me to write this book. In teaching constitutional history, I try to remind my students — and myself — that although "great" cases may enunciate important legal principles, they start with people, men and women who for one reason or another believe they have not been treated rightly and who appeal to the law for help.

Brown v. Board of Education (1954) pronounced the great principle that segregation in public schools is constitutionally wrong; it started with a little girl in the Topeka school system, Linda Brown.

Gideon v. Wainwright (1963) assured all Americans that if any one of them were ever faced by a criminal prosecution, they would have access to an attorney regardless of their finances. That noble idea is written into the Bill of Rights, but it is a reality and not just a platitude because of a rather unlikely and scruffy fellow, Clarence Earl Gideon.

Whether *Johnson v. Transportation Agency, Santa Clara County* ever takes its place among the "great" cases or not, it dealt with an important issue, and we can understand that issue better if we can place it in a human context. That is what I have tried to do in the pages that follow.

Many people helped make my initial idea of a book on *Johnson* into a reality. It has been a real pleasure to work with the staff at the University Press of Kansas, where I've been treated with exceptional professionalism and concern for my needs as an author.

One of my great joys in writing this book is that my son, Robert I. Urofsky, worked with me as a research assistant throughout the project. His questions as we went along, as well as his comments when we were in California, made the work into a joy.

A summer fellowship from the National Endowment for the Humanities provided time for research and writing, and a Littleton-Griswold grant from the American Historical Association helped to underwrite travel costs.

I owe a special debt of thanks to Justice William J. Brennan, Jr., who generously permitted me to examine his office file on *Johnson*.

What made this case important to me were people, and I have tried in the pages that follow to keep their individual stories at the center of the larger tale of the case and of affirmative action. Michael Baratz, Constance Brooks, Charles Fried, James Dawson, David Rosenfeld, Kristine Sermersheim, Suzanne Wilson, and Steven Woodside took the time to sit down and talk with me about their roles in this case. The two key interviews, of course, were with Paul Johnson and Diane Joyce. Both invited me into their homes and spent several hours answering my questions. I made only one promise to all these people — that I would try to tell the story fairly. I hope I have kept that promise.

This book is dedicated to my aunt and my late uncle, who have played such an important role in my own family's life. When my wife Susan and I first embarked on our respective careers, Harry and Shirley provided not only role models but understanding and support for what we were trying to do. Harry was active until his recent death; Shirley is still going strong and showing us the way. They are a tough act to follow.

CHAPTER I

Diane Joyce Makes a Phone Call

Paul Johnson always believed that if you set goals and worked hard, you could achieve them. He had set a goal — the dispatcher's job in the Santa Clara County highway department — and he had worked hard, and soon, his boss told him, the job would be his. Johnson had taken the examination for the job in spring 1980 and placed second among the seven finalists. Under the county rules, the supervisor could choose any one of the top seven; and after a second interview, conducted by the department supervisors, they had made it clear that Paul was their choice. He had been filling in on the job, he was popular with the other workers, and he knew the business; once the paperwork had been taken care of, he would have the dispatcher's mike on a regular basis, with the title and the $480-a-week salary.

Diane Joyce had also been one of the seven finalists, and like Paul Johnson, she also believed that if you worked hard and did the work well, then you ought to be rewarded for your efforts. But as a widow with young children, she found that the best-paying jobs always went to men, and she did not consider that fair. As a clerk in the dispatcher's office, she realized that she could do the dispatcher's job and that it paid a lot more than she would ever make as a clerical worker. To get that post, however, she had to have experience on a road crew, a job no woman had ever held before. Diane forced the road department to hire her, worked on road crews for four years, and took the dispatcher's test at the same time as Paul Johnson. Then she began to hear rumors of a done deal, that the supervisors had already chosen their man, and that she had never had a fair shot at the job. The more she thought about it, the madder she got, until one morning she pulled off on the side of a road, dropped a dime in the telephone, and called the county's affirmative action officer, Helena Lee.

"I'm Diane Joyce," she said. "I'm number four on a list for road dispatcher. No woman has ever held this position before. Are you interested?"

Helena Lee took her name, asked how she could reach her, and said she would be back in touch.

———

Santa Clara County stretches from the southern tip of San Francisco Bay down through one of California's lushest valleys, divided from the Pacific Ocean on the west by the Santa Cruz mountain range. In 1777, Spanish priests raised a cross in a laurel thicket near the Guadalupe River and named it Mission Santa Clara; that same year, settlers built their first homes nearby in the pueblo of San Jose. When California became a state in 1850, Santa Clara served as the first capital, and the region prospered as French settlers planted vineyards in New Almedon. Grain fields gave way to orchards and population grew slowly; at the end of World War II, Santa Clara County had about 290,000 people, most of them engaged in some form of agricultural work. County government was small and simple, and the roads met the needs of the local farmers.

With its mediterranean climate, scenic location, and general prosperity, Santa Clara seemed a wonderful place to live and work. Before long, a lot of people had that idea. The presence of Stanford University at Palo Alto, in the northern part of the county, attracted aerospace and electronics firms, and the sleepy agricultural area soon had another name, Silicon Valley. The 2,600 high-technology companies in the county produced more than 22 percent of American-made electronic computers. County population reached 1.4 million by 1988, with San Jose, the county seat, ranked as the fourteenth largest city in the United States. Companies in and around San Jose produced more than $24.7 billion worth of goods in 1987, the fifth highest in the nation. The comfortable agricultural area had now become a prosperous commercial community, with the highest median family income of any metropolitan area in California; two out of every five households earned $50,000 or more a year.

As the county grew so did county government and the road and transportation system, and much of the political style derived from the highly educated and sophisticated newcomers who flocked to

Silicon Valley. As Suzanne Wilson, a member of the Board of Supervisors, noted:

> You have to look at who came to this valley in the 1950s — engineers. Who did they bring with them, but the kind of women that engineers marry — probably college educated, but also women who were willing to pick up and move, women who had the same sense of adventure and need to expand their horizons.

An "IBM wife" herself, Wilson says that the combination of farmers, blue-collar workers, and educated professionals has created a unique political mix in the county. The people in general are conservative, especially on fiscal matters, but are quite progressive, even liberal, on social issues. A self-described liberal feminist, she has been elected for three terms from the most conservative district in the county.

But liberal or conservative, the county residents have grown used to women in politics, women who "are very outspoken and aggressive in their needs." In 1989, women held three of the five seats on the county Board of Supervisors, and a woman county executive supervised daily affairs; the San Jose City Council had eight women among the eleven members. Perhaps the high percentage of women in local government accounted for the county's early endorsement of an affirmative action plan.

Although affirmative action is normally considered tied to the civil rights movement, blacks constitute only 3.4 percent of Santa Clara County; the two largest minority groups are Hispanics (17.5 percent) and Asians (7.7 percent). From the start, county officials involved with drafting the affirmative action plan, as well as union and citizen groups, had assumed it would apply to women as well as to minorities. Steven Woodside, who would later defend the plan in the Supreme Court, worked on it as a junior county counsel in 1973 and recalled how at the time there had been a lot of discussion in the county about nontraditional jobs for women, job-sharing, and other means of creating opportunities for women. Over the next several years, however, application of the plan appears to have been uneven. Some agency heads made a determined effort to bring in women and minorities; in other departments, the plan might as well not have existed.

The Transportation Agency, for example, like other county units, had its own affirmative action officer in its personnel office, but at least in the highway section, the system had not changed for a long time. As a number of people described it, the road unit had a "good ol' boy" network almost impenetrable to outsiders. Union leader Michael Baratz claimed that

> it's families, all connected, and it's very political. . . . You had to be in the family to get a job, and you found cousins and daughters and sons, and they're all working there. . . . The bottom line is, these guys were racist and sexist. They didn't want women, and they had no intention of ever hiring a woman or a minority person. I'm not saying they were mean-spirited racists. It's just they wanted "one of the boys," somebody they could curse and spit with.

Paul Johnson, in the best sense of the term, was one of the boys, despite the efforts of some people at the time to paint him as a bigoted ogre. His attorney, James Dawson, perhaps caught this quality best when he described Johnson as the sort of man you would like to have as a neighbor — quiet, industrious, and decent. He had been born in 1925 to Kansas farmers who barely eked out a living. His mother was pregnant with her fifth son when his father died of pneumonia. Unable to hold the family together, she parceled Paul, just eight, and the other boys out to various relatives.

He grew up in Gladewater, Texas, and in World War II joined the navy and served on a submarine. After the war he worked as a roustabout, a roughneck, in the oil fields until he married Betty Elliot, with whom he would have three sons. In 1948 they moved to San Jose, and he got a job with Pacific Cement & Aggregate, a construction firm that later became part of Lone Star Industries. He worked for the company seventeen years as a dispatcher and supervisor. In the midsixties the company transferred him to their Oakland facility, at a higher salary and with the potential for promotion. The Johnsons by this time owned their home in San Jose and did not want to uproot their three sons from the local school. For a few months Paul commuted more than four hours a day, a situation that he and his family found very stressful, so he looked around closer to home. With the building boom in Santa Clara County, the Public Works Department, as it was then known, gladly hired a man familiar with road construction.

He began as a Road Yard Clerk II in the East Yard in 1967, with responsibility for requisitioning and purchasing materials for county road construction and maintenance, including road surfacing materials, signs, and concrete culverts. In emergencies, he had the task of finding whatever equipment and supplies might be needed and making sure they got to the site. He occupied an office adjacent to the East Yard dispatcher and would occasionally fill in if the regular dispatcher took a break or was out sick or on vacation.

In 1979, the county reclassified the clerical positions, and as part of a general reorganization, downgraded Johnson's position and reduced the salary. Realizing that he had no chance for advancement unless he changed jobs, Johnson requested reassignment as a Road Maintenance Worker II. The road maintenance category had several levels and could also lead to other higher paying jobs, such as dispatcher. In fact, Johnson had already taken the dispatcher's test once in 1974 and had qualified. Another person, Ron Neal, had been appointed and had been in the job for five years before being promoted to road foreman.

So in 1979 the dispatcher's job opened again, and this time Paul Johnson felt confident he would be the next dispatcher. "I had almost twenty years experience . . . and I knew there was no one else taking the test that was anywhere near qualified as I was." For one thing, he had in effect been the acting dispatcher ever since Neal had been promoted; personnel rules allowed people to "work out of class" temporarily until openings could be filled through the regular hiring procedures. "Usually, if you're doing the job, you automatically get it." Johnson also believed that "99 percent" of his co-workers and his supervisors supported him.

When Johnson had applied for the dispatcher's job in 1974, the procedures called for a written test. This time candidates sat for an oral board, where people from outside the department would examine them on their knowledge and demeanor, asking questions such as "If you were faced with this type of problem, what would you do?" Twelve applicants originally applied; seven of them scored over seventy to qualify for the position. Under the county's personnel policies, a "rule of seven" applied; the hiring supervisor could choose any one of the seven people in the final pool. The Transportation Agency, however, also had a second, informal, oral interview with departmental supervisors. Johnson scored a seventy-five on the first board, although that was not the highest score. After the second board, Bert Di Basilio, the general superintendent, told Johnson that its members had strongly endorsed him and that the job would soon be his; a few days later he found out otherwise.

———

Paul Johnson fit in easily to the camaraderie of the road yard; Diane Joyce did not. Born in Chicago in 1937, the only child of union stalwarts, she learned early on that she had to stand up for her rights; she also learned that in a male-dominated world, life would not always be fair. After a brief stint at the University of Illinois, she took a test for a computer programmer trainee and scored well but was told that the company hired only men for those jobs. Another lesson she learned was that when she did stand up for her rights, not everyone would cheer.

Married at eighteen and eventually the mother of four children, she went back to work in 1958 when her husband Donald, a factory hand, was laid off during the recession. When he did find a job, he told her to quit, but she refused. Donald stormed into an attorney's office, only to learn that employment did not constitute grounds for a divorce. He eventually accepted the situation, and Diane continued to work. She had seven years seniority as an account clerk at the Triner Scale Company when the firm hired a man to do part of her job, and paid him thirty-five dollars a week more. When she asked why, they told her that she had a husband to support her. A year later, in 1969, Donald Joyce died, and Diane decided to move to California. "I wasn't afraid to go out there on my own," she recalled. "I had a trade, and I knew everybody in California needed a bookkeeper."

She rented a house in Santa Clara and got a clerical job with the county's education office, at $506 a month. In early 1972 she heard of a vacancy for a senior account clerk in the Transportation Agency that paid fifty dollars more a month, a lot of money for a widow with small children. Although the hiring supervisors told her they preferred a man, the job had recently been downgraded, and only women applied; Joyce got the job. For a few months, she kept quiet, but she saw that women had most of the clerical jobs while men had the better-paying road jobs. She also watched what the dispatcher did and said to herself, "I can do that, it's not that hard, and he makes $5,000 a year more than I do." When the dispatcher's job came open in 1974, she applied, only to be told that she needed road crew experience.

Joyce calls the requirement for road crew experience an "artificial barrier." Johnson had no road crew experience, yet the county accepted his application and never said a word about road work. As for the job itself, both Joyce and Johnson admit that a good part of the work is clerical and that the most important part is knowing about what sort of equipment and materials are needed for different jobs. She began to pick up the information, and before long she, too, filled in when the dispatcher at her yard went on break. Unlike Paul Johnson, however, she never got assigned to work as a dispatcher out of class.

Whether the requirement was an artificial barrier or not, Joyce realized that she would have to get the road crew experience if she ever hoped to become a dispatcher. As she filled out an application at her desk, her supervisor came in.

"What are you doing?" he asked.

"Applying for a road maintenance man."

"Don't you realize that you're taking a man's job away?" he shouted.

Joyce had been listening to this all her life and had finally had enough.

"No, I'm not," she replied, "because a man can sit right here where I'm sitting."

She took evening courses on road maintenance and light equipment and scored an eighty-seven on the test, coming in third. The county had ten vacancies, and she got one of them. For the next four years she worked on road crews, and although she says that she "had a ball" and that the men on the gangs treated her well, she also tells stories of constant harassment from some of her co-workers as well as from her supervisors. The men on the road crews, for example, were normally assigned coveralls; she had to file a complaint before the agency would issue coveralls to her. On the road crews, bosses routinely assigned her the dull task of handling the Caution paddle and would not let her shovel or handle the equipment. One day on a short crew she got the paddle, but there were not enough men to shovel the asphalt and rake it while it was still hot and malleable. Out of necessity the boss had to let her shovel that day, but as soon as he had a full crew she went back to the paddle.

She had learned from her parents that strong unions can protect their members from management persecution. Joyce joined Local 715 of the Service Employees' International Union (SEIU) and quickly became a leading figure in union activities. Her co-workers, even if they resented her presence on the road crews, recognized her intelligence and elected her shop steward. "I got to do the dishes," she explained. "I think they saw I was intelligent. I think they saw I knew the rules, and I think they saw I could do a good job. And they being basically a very lazy bunch, I was a natural."

She certainly knew the rules and realized that if a harassing practice violated the union's contract, she could file a grievance and be protected from overt retaliation. One time her supervisor reprimanded her in writing for an alleged safety violation, even though normally a first or minor violation triggered only an informal verbal counseling. Joyce then found that there had been six accidents in the previous six months caused by unsafe practices, in which people had been injured, and not one of the *men* had been given even a verbal warning.

When she complained to the supervisor, he grinned and asked, "What are you going to do about it?"

"I'm going to grieve it."

"Aha, you can't," he gloated, "you can't grieve safety."

"Watch me," she shot back.

Joyce had helped negotiate the last union contract, and although a worker could not grieve a safety reprimand, she could grieve harassment. When her case reached the hearing stage, the personnel officer asked her what she wanted.

"Simple. Either all six of those guys who got hurt because of safety violations get written reprimands, or tear mine up."

The hearing officer looked at the supervisor, who recognized that writing post hoc reprimands would make him look bad; he resentfully agreed to tear up Diane Joyce's.

Joyce's role as a union shop steward endeared her to the union officials, one reason they came to her defense later on in the case. But it did not endear her to the supervisors, or to the men in the yards who opposed the union, such as Paul Johnson. Although road workers had been among the founders of the county employees union, many of them either did not want any union at all or perceived SEIU as a "women's union" and wanted to be associated with the Teamsters or the Operating Engineers.

Johnson, according to one union official, was the acknowledged leader of a cadre of anti-union stalwarts. He once came to a union meeting in the yard with a sandwich board saying "I Hate Local 715." The union's contract with the county gave it the right to have bulletin boards in all county offices, where news of union activities could be posted. Paul Johnson, with at least the tacit endorsement of his supervisor, put up his own bulletin board, and there he would tack up newspaper clippings of union leaders getting arrested or accounts of union funds embezzled.

———

Looking back later, Diane Joyce could not believe how naive she had been at the time and that she had not recognized that the yard bosses had already chosen Paul Johnson. She began to hear stories that Johnson had been selected, but "I didn't want to believe them." Then she got a card informing her that she had qualified for the dispatcher's post and that she should call Bert Di Basilio, the general superintendent, to arrange for an interview with the informal board. She called Di Basilio to tell him that she did want the job; then, according to the procedures, he should have informed her within three days when the interview had been scheduled.

Ten days passed, and Joyce still had not heard anything, so on a Friday afternoon she drove over to the East Yard where Di Basilio had his office. She told him that she hoped the interview would not be set up for the following Tuesday, since she had a four-hour disaster preparedness class that morning, part of her responsibilities as safety steward for the West Yard. Di Basilio told her he did not know when it would be. The following Monday when she got back to the yard after work on the roads, she found a note that the interview would be the following morning at 10:00, right in the middle of her class. As Joyce laconically noted, "It's hard for me to believe that's just coincidental." That "coincidence," together with the rumors she had been hearing that Paul Johnson already had the job sewed up, led her to take action and call the affirmative action officer.

Following her interview with the superintendents, nothing happened. "I don't hear anything for three weeks," she later recalled. "Not a word. Nobody calls me back, but there's no announcement [that Johnson got the job]. So I knew something was up. . . . And I thought, the longer it takes, the better off I'll be." But even during these three weeks, she did not believe she would actually get the job. The affirmative action office, as she well knew, did not have any power to make appointments. In fact, unbeknownst to her, the affirmative action people had begun looking into her case right after she had called them, and in a very effective manner.

Normally, the responsibility for hiring a dispatcher would rest with the supervisor for road operations, a man named Ron Shields, who not only thought well of Paul Johnson but also had already had several run-ins with Diane Joyce. Once he made his decision, it required routine approval from James Graebner, the director of the Transportation Agency. Before Shields could get that approval, the county affirmative action office notified Victor Morton, the Transportation Agency's affirmative action coordinator, about Diane Joyce's telephone call, and he immediately went to see Graebner. As Graebner later testified at the trial,

> [Morton] just walked into the office one day and said, "Hey, this is a promotional opportunity, and you need to know about it." Mr. Morton was less interested in the particular individual; he felt that this was an opportunity for us to take a step toward meeting our affirmative action goals, and because there was only one person on the list who was one of the protected groups, he felt that this afforded us an opportunity to meet those goals through the appointment of that member of a protected group.

Graebner did not consider the appointment a major issue; in fact, had it not been for Morton suggesting that choosing Diane Joyce would help implement the affirmative action plan, he would never have involved himself in a routine, low-level appointment. Once Morton assured him that both Joyce and Johnson had qualified for the job, he did not even bother calling for their files. Under the rule of seven, any of the seven qualified candidates could be named. Graebner had no problems with the idea of affirmative action or with appointing a woman to a job never before held by a female. And as he quite openly admitted, Joyce's gender not only had been a positive factor, it had been the main factor leading to her selection.

Despite arguments from Shields that Johnson ought to get the job, Graebner stuck to his decision, and Bert Di Basilio had to tell Paul Johnson. He called Johnson into his office and said, "I've got some bad news for you. You did not get the job."

Astonished, Johnson exclaimed, "You must be kidding."

"No," said Di Basilio, "Diane Joyce was appointed. You had already been appointed, and affirmative action got it reversed."

Di Basilio assured Johnson that he had done everything that he could have in his behalf but that the matter was out of his hands.

Paul Johnson "felt like tearing something up." He knew Diane Joyce and believed then and later that he had the better qualifications for the job. "But she wanted a middle-level position right off, without having to work for it like I did. I would never ask for preferential treatment, and that's what she was doing."

Johnson determined to fight right from the start, and since the system had always worked for him before, he would give it one more chance and go through the channels. He spoke with supervisors Allen Jones and Ron Shields, and they more or less repeated with Di Basilio had said, that he had been their choice, he had been named dispatcher, and then Graebner had given the job to Joyce. Johnson then called Graebner's office for an appointment. Graebner's secretary asked what he wanted to discuss, and when Johnson told her the dispatcher's job, she told him he would have to see Victor Morton first. She then transferred the call to the affirmative action coordinator, who told Johnson he could meet with him that afternoon.

"If it was in any way close," Johnson later said, "I wouldn't have any problem." Di Basilio, Jones, and Shields, men who had been his bosses and whose judgment he respected, had told him that it had not been close, that he had far better qualifications than Diane Joyce. At this point, still believing in the system, Paul Johnson wanted someone to tell him that there had been a rational reason why he had not been given the job.

Victor Morton did not give him that reason. Johnson met with Morton and his assistant and asked Morton if he could explain how he could make an appointment like that, or even recommend it. "Well," Morton said, "your qualifications are very similar."

Johnson immediately challenged that and asked Morton to show him how the records justified such a conclusion. Morton did not have any records with him, and an exasperated Johnson nearly exploded. "Well, what do you think I wanted to talk to you about?"

In an effort to calm Johnson down, Morton tried to explain that he did not control the appointment process but merely had made a recommendation to the agency head. He had done so because, in accordance with the affirmative action plan, they wanted to put a woman in a position that no woman had ever held before.

When Johnson met with Graebner a little while later, the Transportation Agency chief told him essentially the same thing — he considered both applicants evenly matched, but he wanted to use the opportunity to put a woman into the position. Johnson angrily asked what Graebner intended to do about the merit system — "just throw it out the damn window?" Graebner did not comment, and Johnson went home to think about his next step.

———

Betty Johnson felt as outraged as her husband. Paul had worked hard, he had demonstrated his competence, he had played by the rules — and now they had unfairly changed the rules. When she told her brother-in-law about Paul's problem, he told her that he knew someone on the San Jose police force who had been denied a promotion because of affirmative action and had successfully sued in court. He recommended contacting the law firm that had handled the policeman's case, Wiley, Blunt & McBride, one of the first firms in the Santa Clara area to handle labor law. Johnson called their office, and the switchboard put him through to one of the junior associates, James Dawson.

Dawson had worked for Legal Services after law school and had gradually come to specialize in employment discrimination cases. Johnson came in to see him and explained the situation. Affirmative action had stopped his appointment, Johnson claimed, and this violated the county's rules for nonrepresented employees. Could anything be done?

Dawson said, "I don't know; let's write a letter." Acting on behalf of Johnson, Dawson wrote to Jim Graebner, asking for an opportunity to discuss Paul Johnson's complaint prior to invoking the county grievance procedure. Graebner did not respond. Acting through Dawson, Johnson next filed a claim with the Equal Employment Opportunity Commission (EEOC).

These actions, it should be noted, took place in the three weeks following Diane Joyce's telephone call in spring 1980. Bert Di Basilio finally called her in to Room 8 at the West Yard, a room normally reserved for disciplinary meetings, and said, "Well, you got it."

"Great," she responded. "What did I get?"

"The East Yard road dispatchership. You and your friends got you the dispatcher's job."

Joyce, who up until then had not really believed she would get the position, suddenly realized what Di Basilio had said and exclaimed, "Fantastic!"

Di Basilio did not think it so fantastic. "You got it through affirmative action, even though you were not qualified."

"What do you mean, not qualified? I was number four on the certification list. I'm certified to the department. That makes me qualified."

"Well, not as qualified as Paul Johnson." And he told her about the rankings.

———

As Diane Joyce prepared to take over the dispatcher's job in East Yard in June 1980, the local EEOC office invited the county to meet with Jim Dawson in an effort to resolve the dispute. The county ignored this letter as well, and EEOC then had a choice of what to do next. One option would be to follow regular administrative procedure and send out "requests for information." The aggrieved party in a complicated case may often prefer this route, since it is a cheap method of discovery, that is, of getting information from the employer's records that can be used in building one's own case. But Dawson believed he had a solid, straightforward case and that the county had delayed long enough. He wanted to get into court and to force Santa Clara County to do right by Paul Johnson.

So he invoked another option and secured a "right to sue" letter from the EEOC. Such a letter implies no guilt but indicates that there is a potential violation of the law amenable to suit in federal court. Without the right to sue letter, Paul Johnson could not go forward.

With it, Jim Dawson filed papers in the U.S. District Court for the Northern District of California, alleging that the county's action had violated Title VII of the 1964 Civil Rights Act, 42 U.S.C. § 2000e, which prohibits discrimination on the basis of gender.

The court had a crowded docket, and Paul Johnson would have to wait almost two years before Judge William A. Ingram would hear the case. During that time, Diane Joyce ran the dispatcher's desk at East Yard, the same yard where Paul Johnson worked as a member of the road crew. During those two years his resentment of her and of affirmative action did not abate at all.

CHAPTER 2

The Debate over Affirmative Action

No aspect of the modern civil rights movement has generated so much heat and so little agreement as affirmative action. Its advocates claim that setting goals for the admission of minorities and women into colleges, training programs, and employment will eventually move these groups out of second-class status and give them true equality in American life. Opponents believe quotas that favor one group must inevitably discriminate against another and lead to the hiring of lesser qualified minorities and women at the expense of better qualified white males, who themselves are not guilty of discrimination. The debate has raised many questions about whether affirmative action in fact works, and if it does, who benefits and at whose expense.

Following the Civil War, Congress passed a number of laws designed to put the former slaves on a rough par with white people. The Fourteenth Amendment made the freedmen citizens and prohibited states from enforcing any law that abridged the privileges and immunities of any citizen, deprived them of life, liberty, or property without due process of law, or denied them the equal protection of the laws. It also gave Congress the power to enforce these provisions, and in 1875 the Republican majority in Congress, aware that Reconstruction would soon end, passed a Civil Rights Act to secure by law some semblance of equality for black Americans.

It is doubtful if many white Americans really endorsed the idea of equality for the freedmen. Gideon Welles, who had been secretary of the navy in Lincoln's cabinet, captured the prevailing sentiment when he wrote in 1871: "Thank God slavery is abolished, but the Negro is not, and never can be the equal of the White. He is of an inferior race and must always remain so." The Supreme Court agreed and in 1883 emasculated the postwar statutes and diluted much of the protection of the Fourteenth Amendment. In the *Civil Rights Cases* Justice Joseph Bradley interpreted the enforcement provisions of the amendment as strictly remedial; Congress had the power to remedy a discriminatory state law but could not take affirmative steps to protect blacks from other forms of prejudice.

As a result of this decision, the federal government took no action to combat racism in this country until World War II, when it became embarrassing to claim we were fighting racism abroad while tolerating it at home. Black resentment became more vocal, and to forestall threatened civil rights demonstrations, including a march on Washington, Pres. Franklin D. Roosevelt issued an executive order on June 25, 1941, directing that Negroes be accepted into job-training programs in defense plants. The order also forbade discrimination by employers holding defense contracts and set up a Fair Employment Practices Commission to investigate charges of racial discrimination. After the war Congress proved unwilling to enact fair employment legislation, but Harry Truman and Dwight Eisenhower both continued Roosevelt's policy through executive order.

Following the Supreme Court decision in *Brown v. Board of Education* in 1954, pressure mounted on Congress and the executive to take some positive steps on behalf of civil rights. John F. Kennedy entered the White House in January 1961 amid high hopes from blacks that he would provide the moral leadership that had been so painfully absent during the Eisenhower years. Roy Wilkins of the NAACP called for immediate action to promote employment opportunities for Negroes, and the new president responded with Executive Order 10925, creating a presidential Commission on Equal Employment Opportunity and mandating federal contractors to take "affirmative action" to ensure that there be no discrimination by "race, creed, color or national origin." For the first time, the government ordered its contractors not only to avoid discrimination but also to take positive steps to redress the effects of societal discrimination.

Kennedy realized that an executive order could go only so far and that real progress in civil rights required congressional action. In 1963 he secured passage of the Equal Pay Act, which prohibited employers from paying women less than men for the same work. He also proposed sweeping civil rights legislation, which southerners managed to bottle up in committee. After Kennedy's assassination, however, Lyndon Johnson called for the passage of the civil rights bill as a memorial to the slain president, and he skillfully guided an expanded version of the Kennedy proposal through both houses of Congress, broke a southern filibuster, and signed the Civil Rights Act into law on July 2, 1964. Title VII of the act banned employment discrimination based on "race, color, sex or national origin" and created a Permanent Equal Employment Opportunity Commission to enforce its provisions. The act extended for the first time the obligation not to discriminate to private employers, labor unions, and governmental agencies.

Despite the sweeping language of the act, very little progress occurred, and within a short time Johnson realized that merely banning current discrimination was not enough; something had to be done for blacks to overcome the lingering effects of decades of systematic exclusion from jobs and education. In a speech at Howard University, Johnson explained why the country needed to adopt affirmative action:

> You do not take a person who for years has been hobbled by chains, and liberate him, bring him up to the starting line of a race, and then say, "You are free to compete with all the others," and still justly believe that you have been completely fair. Thus, it is not enough just to open the gates of opportunity, all our citizens must have the ability to walk through those gates.

In Executive Order 11246, issued on September 24, 1965, Johnson required federal contractors to take affirmative action to recruit, hire, and promote more minorities. Two years later, in Executive Order 11375, Johnson added women to the groups covered by previous antidiscrimination orders.

Johnson's vision, however, soon bogged down in the Great Society bureaucracy. Affirmative action, according to some critics, became an umbrella term for a vast hodgepodge of remedial programs, ranging from efforts to place more women on university faculties to hiring more blacks in the construction industry. Over a dozen federal agencies shared responsibility for enforcing two dozen equal opportunity laws or executive orders; these agencies overlapped in some areas and left huge gaps in others. In an effort to plug all loopholes, zealous bureaucrats drew up seemingly endless forms and regulations, whose net effect, if any, no one seemed to know.

When Richard Nixon took office in 1969, he faced on the one hand a growing backlash by blue-collar whites against civil rights and on the other the realization that many of the economic problems associated with welfare and big cities stemmed from the job discrimination confronting black Americans. Compliance with Title VII still remained voluntary, and most American businesses had chosen to wait and see what they would be required to do instead of initiating any programs on their own. Nixon, with prompting from domestic affairs adviser Daniel Patrick Moynihan, accepted the idea that blacks had to be brought into the economic mainstream or they would never escape the chains of poverty and discrimination that had bound them since the chains of slavery had been struck off.

The president called in Art Fletcher, the assistant secretary of labor and a black himself, and told him to find a way to enforce the hiring provisions of Title VII, a way that would withstand court challenge. Fletcher did, and in 1971 Nixon unveiled the so-called Philadelphia Plan, a model for bringing minorities into segregated trades. In Philadelphia federal contractors would have to meet specific numerical goals in hiring minorities, with the long-term goal equaling the percentage of that minority in the available labor force. The Nixon plan, issued as the Office of Federal Contract Compliance (OFCC) Revised Order No. 4, strengthened the two Johnson orders by requiring annual affirmative action plans from major contractors as well as hiring goals and timetables. According to Fletcher, the Nixon administration ordered what Congress had not, numerical goals and enforcement. In the next eighteen months Fletcher toured the country urging blacks to take advantage of the new order. "I went to wherever I could get a platform," he later recalled, "to make sure that everyone understood that this standard required that you be prepared to make a contribution. . . . It is not a futile effort anymore. The door is open."

Fletcher provided a walking case in point of what circumstances had been like for blacks in the 1950s. He had graduated from college in 1950, played professional football for a few years, and then could not get a job. He went back to his native Kansas and could not even get hired as an assistant coach in high school. People told him, "You are ready, but we are not." So Fletcher worked as an ice man, ran a janitorial service, and played trumpet on weekends to support his wife and five children. He moved to California in 1956 where Republican party leaders welcomed him into their ranks and appointed him to some legislative advisory groups. Nonetheless, as Fletcher later told a reporter, it took him fifteen years to find a job that required his college degree. By then he had moved to the state of Washington and had become the first black to run for statewide office. Although Fletcher lost the bid for the lieutenant governorship in 1968, he caught the attention of national party leaders, and Nixon named him to the Labor Department in his new administration.

The plan Fletcher designed, with its innovation of goals and time-tables, soon caught the attention of frustrated federal judges looking for ways to force recalcitrant public employers to integrate their work force. A good case in point was Alabama, where more than seventy state agencies employed only a handful of blacks above the menial level. In January 1972 the NAACP sued the Alabama state police, which did not have a single black among its troopers, officers, or even support personnel. Federal Judge Frank M. Johnson, Jr., imposed a rule that one black trooper had to be hired for every new white person hired, until 25 percent of the force consisted of blacks. Twelve years later, the state had the most thoroughly integrated state-police force in the country.

The Nixon order also proved the turning point for private employers. Businesses do not deal well with vague generalities, but they do respond to specifics. As one article put it, "Businessmen like to hire by the numbers." Once they had something specific to work with, hundreds, indeed thousands of firms began the often painful process of self-examination, of looking at their past hiring practices and recognizing that they had, consciously or not, excluded minorities from employment and promotion. In little more than a decade, affirmative action became a way of life for many large corporations. Once embarked on the program, primarily through fear of losing lucrative federal contracts, corporations began discovering, or at least rationalizing, other reasons for their policies. Marion Sandler of Golden West Financial explained that "the whole country is moving away from being white, Anglo and Protestant to polyglot," especially in places like California and Texas where Golden West did business. "You have to recognize what's happening and be part of it." John M. Stafford, head of the Pillsbury Company, shared this sentiment. "It has become clear to us that an aggressive affirmative action program makes a lot of sense."

A 1983 survey of fifty major federal contractors conducted for the Center for National Policy Review indicated that all had accepted affirmative action as "an integral part of today's corporate personnel-management philosophy and practice." B. Lawrence Branch, the director of equal employment for the Merck Company, admitted that the pharmaceutical firm would not have initiated an affirmative action plan without the government's prodding but that now "we don't need the government involved in this—affirmative action is a way of life here."

One should not suppose that all American businesses endorsed the philosophy behind affirmative action or that, on the other hand, they went along only out of fear of losing government contracts. In fact, the threat of federal retaliation has always been more potential than actual. As Alan Farnham noted, a quarter-century after the Civil Rights Act:

> The mortar binding CEOs to affirmative action—a compound of social conscience, fear, and self-interest—appears strong. Some CEOs believe fervently that the programs are the best way of righting past wrongs. Others half-heartedly endorse them because, like eating oatmeal, it's the right thing to do. Still others fear the penalties for backsliding.

———

That thousands of firms initiated affirmative action programs is indisputable; how much these programs helped minorities and women is greatly disputed. It is impossible to get accurate figures because in many instances blacks and other minorities might have been hired even in the absence of an affirmative action plan. The best numbers come from those firms or agencies that had admittedly discriminated in the past and where blacks or women entered the job force only because of affirmative action. There is no question that these plans helped some talented individuals who might not otherwise have had a chance. Art Fletcher claims that one-third of black Americans used the civil rights acts and presidential orders "to position themselves in middle class America. One-third of black America has made it within the last twenty years — the life of this document, affirmative action." The only ones who did not make it, he charges, are those who did not try.

Not everyone agrees. Thomas Sowell, a senior fellow at the Hoover Institution, argues that affirmative action has not helped the people who need help most, those with little education, training, or job experience; rather, it has benefited the top 10 percent poised to move into the middle class in any event. Affirmative action "may help a black professor get an endowed chair, but it is counter-productive for the black teenager trying to get a job." Other critics, including sociologist Nathan Glazer and Douglas Glasgow, author of *The Black Underclass* (1980), have indicted affirmative action for failing to help the mass of poor blacks.

One can certainly find success stories. Earl Jenkins is now a national marketing manager for AT&T, overseeing 100 people and an annual budget of $25 million, and believes that without affirmative action, he would never have had the opportunity to demonstrate his ability. AT&T recruited Jenkins, a black man, in 1975 under a consent decree with the EEOC. In 1969 blacks made up 6.7 percent of the nearly 600,000 employees in the Bell system, mostly black women working as operators, but only 2.4 percent of black employees held management positions, compared to 12 percent of whites. Less than 1 percent of the blacks held professional jobs, compared to 8 percent of the whites.* In 1971 the EEOC charged AT&T and its affiliates with discrimination against blacks and women, and the consent decree signed four years later became the catalyst for rapid change within the giant telephone system. By 1979 blacks and other minorities made up 14.4 percent of the Bell system's managers, 18.7 percent of its outside

---

* By way of comparison to the total work force, in 1988 there were 182,628,000 Americans aged eighteen and over, the group that statistically constitutes the work force. Of these, 78.6 percent were white, 11.2 percent black, 7.1 percent Hispanic, and 3.1 percent "other," a group that includes Asians, Native Americans, and other small minorities, such as Aleuts. By gender, the population is 51.2 percent female and 48.8 percent male.

craftsmen, and 23.3 percent of its salesworkers. The talent had been there all along; employers had not looked for it.

Similar stories can be told about minority experiences in other firms and industries, and how affirmative action opened doors previously closed to blacks and women. Coal mining, for example, had traditionally been a male industry, and there were no women miners in 1973. The EEOC targeted the coal industry as one of several whose hiring policies flagrantly violated the letter and the spirit of the presidential orders. By the end of 1980, 3,295 women had become coal miners, 8.7 percent of the total work force. Similarly, the number of women in shipbuilding increased dramatically when the Maritime Administration required contractors to establish goals and timetables. Although many shipyard owners had claimed women had no interest in shipbuilding, they found that as more women were hired, more applied. The Wilson Meat Company of Cedar Rapids, Iowa, proudly declared that it had the only woman hog buyer in the country but admitted that a few years earlier it would never have even considered a female for that job. The Office of Federal Contract Compliance believed that in certain "hardcore" industries such as construction, "unless specific affirmative action steps are prescribed, employment opportunities will not reach the female work force of this country." Several studies support the claim that affirmative action does provide minorities and women with equal employment opportunity. Perhaps the most visibly successful affirmative action programs are those of the armed services, which in a relatively short period of time brought in large numbers of women and minorities not only to the army, navy, and air force but also to the respective service academies as well.

After Indianapolis instituted hiring goals in 1976, black representation on its police force rose to 14 percent. Barry Goldstein of the NAACP Legal Defense Fund noted that in 1970 there were about 23,000 black police officers in the country; in 1979 there were 43,000; in that same decade, the number of black electricians rose from 15,000 to more than 37,000. For him, numbers such as these proved that affirmative action worked.

Critics of affirmative action have their own numbers to show that the programs have not worked that well and have not helped more than a small number of people. Thus, for example, in 1970, 31.5 million women held jobs, and they earned on the whole only 59.2

percent of men's salaries. In 1985 the number of working women had grown to 51.1 million, and the salary gap had closed somewhat to 65 percent. A breakdown of those numbers, however, indicated that white women entering the job market in 1980 were actually further behind the wages of comparable white men than they had been in 1970, despite the alleged success of affirmative action. A 1985 study by the National Research Council reported that sex segregation in employment had remained fairly stable since 1900. Despite some changes after 1975, the segregation index still remained at 60, which meant that 30 percent of workers would have to move into job categories dominated by the opposite sex just to even the numbers out. Moreover, in its study, the council found that overall, women still earned only 60 percent as much as men.

———

The debate, however, is not over numbers; it is over social philosophy, and what the nation as a whole should do in its efforts to eradicate race and gender discrimination. In its bluntest form, the argument for affirmative action is this: past discrimination in the job market has placed minorities and women at a disadvantage that will never, left to itself, go away. Minorities and women will always be in an inferior position unless steps are taken to pull them up. This circumstance requires some temporary discrimination against white males, but it is necessary for the sake of social justice and progress. As McGeorge Bundy acknowledged:

> The reason is simple, it is also painful: the gaps in economic, educational, and cultural advantage between racial minorities and the white majority are still so wide that *there is no racially neutral process of choice that will produce more than a handful of minority students in our competitive colleges and professional schools.* . . . Precisely because it is not yet "racially neutral" to be black in America, a racially neutral standard will not lead to equal opportunity for blacks.

In other words, to compensate for past injustice, there must be a form of reverse discrimination now. One economist described the position of blacks and other minorities as comparable to a caboose on a train. "No matter how fast the train goes, the caboose will never catch up with the engine unless special arrangements are made to change its position." Minorities and women will always be at the tail end of the economy and even in good times will always trail after the white majority — unless affirmative action provides them with greater opportunities.

Ralph F. Davidson, chairman of the board of Time, Inc., despaired for the future of the country unless something could be done to break "the treadmill of underemployment and joblessness, of opportunities forever beyond reach." Affirmative action, he believed, constituted one of the few "proved and practical means" to help people stand on their own feet. Only by giving minorities this opportunity, according to columnist Charles Krauthammer, would the country ever have a chance of fully integrating blacks into American life.

Another argument put forward in defense of affirmative action is that the country cannot afford to waste the talents of people who, because of their race, gender, or national origin, would be prevented from realizing their potential. "How am I," asked Health, Education, and Welfare (HEW) Secretary Joseph A. Califano, "ever going to find first-class black doctors, first-class black lawyers, first-class black scientists, first-class women scientists, if these people don't have the chance to get into the best [schools] in the country?" These professionals will also serve the needs of their respective communities, which presently are underserved in terms of medical and legal services. Minority doctors, according to one study, are more likely to care for poor and minority patients and to practice in ghetto areas than white doctors.

Educators have claimed that affirmative action is needed not only for the benefit of minorities and women but also to provide the schools, and their white students, the benefit of a student population reflective of the outside society. The dean of Columbia College, Robert Pollack, described affirmative action as justice, not charity:

I despair at how vulnerable our affirmative action policies are to the short-term politics of the day. To lose sight of the distinction between charity and justice is to promulgate injustice in the name of fiscal responsibility, and to condemn our white classmates and colleagues to intellectual ghettoes of their own making. . . .

Each year we seek out black and Latin candidates for admission to the College. We show underrepresented minority candidates and their families the ins and outs of life in this diverse but still largely white institution. . . . The impetus of all our recruiting programs is the same: to bring to the College the most diverse possible group of students with high intelligence and character.

This last phrase, "students with high intelligence and character," involves another argument for affirmative action, that it is not a lowering of standards but an opportunity to involve skilled and talented people who would otherwise be excluded from attending certain schools or securing certain jobs. McGeorge Bundy denied that anyone wanted to admit unqualified students; rather, "there are qualified minorities, and they need a boost." Some studies, however, show that many colleges deliberately lowered admission standards for certain groups in order to increase their percentage of minority students.

The issue of whether persons benefited by affirmative action have the necessary qualifications, be they for a job or for admission to college, ties in closely to whether one views affirmative action programs as setting out *goals* or *quotas*. Advocates argue that setting goals is acceptable; we set goals in our lives, businesses set goals for sales and production, and nations can also set goals toward which to strive. To try to shape one's work force or student body so that it roughly corresponds to the general population is a worthy goal and discriminates against no one. To set a specific number of blacks or women or Hispanics, however, is a quota, and critics charge that quotas do discriminate against nonfavored groups and that often an unqualified person is hired or admitted so that the quotas can be filled.

Reams of paper have been written on the distinction between goals and quotas. Eugene Rostow, when asked how the two differed, said that one meets goals in affirmative action plans by recruiting women, blacks, and other minorities "where there simply has been no history of hiring such people." The editors of *Commonweal* spoke of casting a "wide net" in which "job training efforts and serious attempts at remedial education can well be seen as indications of good intentions that make imposition of a quota system unnecessary."

In other words, one opens the door wider, and invites — indeed seeks out — people who previously have either been turned away or led to believe they would be unwelcome to apply. Then, by the natural distribution of talent and ability, those people chosen will include women and minorities. As a result, the overall pool potential of students or employees expands to include more qualified people, and those chosen will, as a group, have a higher level of ability.

The problem is, as critics claim and some friends admit, it does not work this way. Setting goals and timetables at some point fades into setting quotas. It is all too easy to go from saying, "We should have 10 percent blacks or 50 percent women, and that is the goal we should work toward by active recruitment and training," to saying, "The next thirty people we hire must be black or female so we meet our quota." As then Attorney General Edward H. Levi charged in 1975, affirmative action programs established goals that were "said with great profoundness not to be the setting of quotas. But it is the setting of quotas . . . [even though] we will call quotas goals." And goals do discriminate, because in order to fill the quota, one will hire people if they are female or black or the member of another minority even if they are less qualified than available white males.

To some advocates of affirmative action, quotas are acceptable. Arthur Fleming, the chair of the U.S. Commission on Civil Rights, asserted in a 1981 report that sometimes "quotas are needed to make equal opportunity a reality for members of historically excluded groups." Merely opening the doors wider will do no good, runs the argument, because the same prejudice that barred minorities from getting these jobs also worked to provide them with inferior education and training. John Fischer, former dean of Columbia Teachers College, said of a typical black child, "On the day he enters kindergarten, he carries a burden no white child can ever know." Telling an unqualified person who carries such a burden that he or she is free to apply to good schools or for good jobs is a charade. What has to be done is to take members of previously excluded groups and treat them preferentially until such time as they can compete for jobs or places in colleges and medical schools.

The issue here, according to Daniel Maguire, is not fairness or equality but justice. It is true that quotas are unfair and treat people unequally, but we as a society accept certain inequalities because we perceive them as just. "A school that was established to allow unequal and special education for the gifted would not be resented. The handicapped have a right to unequal, extra help from the state." Minorities who have been discriminated against have the right to expect not only compensatory programs but some preference as well. Charles Krauthammer makes a similar argument. "While color blindness may be a value, remedying centuries of discrimination through (temporary) race consciousness is a higher value," namely, justice. Moreover, the rapid integration of blacks into American society "is an overriding national goal," and quotas are a means to that goal. That integration, according to affirmative action advocates, will mean not only a more economically productive work force but also less poverty among minorities and a reduction in crime and other social problems that stalk the nation's ghettos.

But what about the white males who will pay the price for these preferential programs, white males who, like Paul Johnson, have never even been accused of personal discrimination? Mayor William Hudnot of Indianapolis, where police and fire departments ran extensive affirmative action programs, said that he did not think that white males suffered greatly, since they still got 80 percent of the jobs in those agencies. According to Ira Glasser, head of the American Civil Liberties Union, whites have enjoyed unfair advantages over blacks, women, and minorities for many years. "Fairness," he argues, "requires ending discrimination, not perpetuating it, and that includes ending the advantages that whites enjoyed."

Key to the question of alleged discrimination against white males is how one views an individual's responsibility for social injustice. Does everyone bear the blame for past racial injustice, prejudice against women, or exclusion of minorities from schools and jobs? Why should a white person whose grandparents came to this country long after slavery had ended have to pay a price for the iniquities inflicted upon blacks by their white masters years earlier? The "just citizen," answers Daniel Maguire, cannot be at peace while social injustice exists. Even if he is guilty of no personal offense,

> he owes a debt to legal justice by the very nature of social personhood. Here the guilt is the guilt of omission, the guilt of not having done enough, of not caring enough. . . . In the matter of American racism, the white who would claim to be without such guilt is, in the phrase and spirit of the Apostle John, "a liar."

Paul Spickard faced a personal test of his commitment to this Christian view of justice. Spickard, a white male, had degrees from

Harvard and Berkeley in Asian history but was twice turned down for jobs because colleges wanted a minority person. "Isn't all this unfair?" he asked. Yes, he concluded, but

> my family came over on the *Mayflower* and made money in the slave trade. Doctors, lawyers, judges and comfortable business people go back several generations in my clan. . . . I am standing on the shoulders of my ancestors and their discriminatory behavior.
>
> Contrast my experience with that of a Chicano friend, whose immigrant father had a fourth-grade education and ran a grocery store. Without affirmative action and the social commitment it symbolizes, my friend might not have gone to Amherst, nor to Stanford Law School. . . . Our society would be poorer for the loss of his skills. . . .
>
> Affirmative action may not always be fair. But I'm willing to take second best if overall fairness is achieved. After all, for biblical Christians, fairness — often translated in our Bibles as "justice" or "righteousness" — is a fundamental principle by which God calls us to live. And affirmative action is an appropriate program aimed at achieving the godly goal of putting other's welfare before my own.

All arguments in favor of affirmative action boil down to the fact that women, blacks, and other minorities have historically suffered discrimination and have been precluded from various educational and economic opportunities. In order for society to eliminate the lasting vestiges of that discrimination and to realize the potential contributions of all its citizens, it has to take certain steps to allow these groups access to good schools and good jobs. Whether one talks of goals or quotas, the aim is the same — admit more members of the excluded groups into schools, hire them into jobs and job-training programs. If in the past, the majority used a person's race or gender or national origin against that person in a discriminatory manner, then now it is fair to take those same considerations into account and to use them to the person's benefit.

———

For critics of affirmative action, race-conscious or gender-conscious programs that benefit minorities are as bad as the discrimination against these groups. Where advocates claim that the programs work, critics say they do not. Moral arguments for are met by equally moral arguments against. Although defenders assert that affirmative action will eventually lead to an America in which minorities and women take their rightful and equal place, critics foresee an even more race- and gender-conscious society.

The nub of the critics' moral argument is that while women, blacks, and other minorities have been discriminated against as *groups*, quotas that benefit these groups disadvantage *individual* white males. Not all white males pay the price of society's desire to compensate victims of past discrimination; only those in targeted jobs or schools. The political philosopher Sidney Hook has agreed that society had in the past immorally discriminated against minorities — blacks, Orientals, Jews, women, and others.

> But it is illiberal and unjust to redress the effects of past discrimination by punishing innocent parties in the present whose ancestors had no part in imposing the patterns of discrimination in the past. If society in the past has been guilty of discrimination, then the costs of reparations should be borne by society as a whole to the extent that there can ever be adequate reparation rather than by innocent persons in the present.

The system, as the then-liberal *New Republic* admitted, cannot be designed so that only "oppressors" are excluded, even if society could identify such people. "The fate of young men and women is at stake, and they are classified according to their racial or ethnic identity, not according to their moral conduct."

Not only is the price paid for by individuals, but most of these individuals come from marginal white groups. Affirmative action rarely affects upper-class white males; they have been well educated and usually have no trouble getting into good colleges, graduate schools, or beginning managerial or professional positions. Rather, it is the marginal candidates, those who have not been as well educated, who themselves may come from poor or disadvantaged backgrounds, who are bumped to make room for women and minorities. The result is that the bottom groups will not be pushed up to an equality with all others but merely pushed ahead of the "next-to-last" group, primarily white ethnic Americans. And that, according to critics, is grossly unfair and simply shifts the injustice to another group, leaving the basic inequalities of American society untouched.

If the programs worked, critics maintain, then there might be grounds for supporting it as an avowed national policy, recognizing that for certain groups to benefit others will have to suffer. Life is unfair, and we have many national policies that benefit one group at the expense of others. But, they claim, affirmative action does not work. Thomas Sowell, one of the most forceful critics of affirmative action, charges that its track record in helping to alleviate social ills is even poorer than busing. Though various programs helped some of the "more fortunate" blacks and women, "the truly disadvantaged — those with little education or job experience, or from broken families — have fallen even further behind during the era of affirmative action."

In fact, Sowell claims, the real gains among blacks in high-level occupations began not with affirmative action or even with the passage of the Civil Rights Act in 1964 but is part of a "historic, ongoing process created by one of the great social transformations of a people." "Don't make things worse," he pleads. The progress of American blacks since emancipation has been "remarkable," but "massive intervention [on their behalf] has had massive counterproductive effects," most notably a swelling white backlash that threatens to unleash new waves of racism.

Sowell does not claim that all racial or sexual discrimination has ended in the United States, but George Gilder, a conservative writer in the *National Review*, does argue along those lines. Affirmative action, he declares, should be stopped not just because it is unconstitutional or unfair to poor white males, "but because discrimination has already been effectively abolished in this country." Since *Brown*, a "relentless and thoroughly successful" campaign against the old prejudices has made it impossible to label modern America as oppressive and discriminatory, with gaps in income between truly comparable blacks and whites "nearly closed."

As for women, Gilder believes that their problems are caused not by gender discrimination but by conditions that can never be changed. Most of the differences in pay are due to the *fact* that women between the ages of twenty-five and fifty-nine are eleven times more likely than men to leave work voluntarily. The average woman spends only eight months on a job, compared to nearly three years for the average man. Lower pay for equal work, he further maintains, "is an effect not of discrimination but of locational preference"; women are less mobile than men because they must live where their husbands work and therefore cannot be as choosy in finding well-paying jobs.

Few people would take such a sanguine view of contemporary American racial or gender conditions, but a number of critics worry that imposing quotas to benefit particular groups could undermine the real progress that has been made. Where, for example, would one draw the line as to what groups should be protected? One finds in a leading news magazine such stories as "Short People — Are They Being Discriminated Against?" and "Fat People's Fight Against Job Bias." A white female office worker, fired after she was caught fornicating on business premises during working hours, filed a discrimination charge against her employer, as did a Caribbean-born stewardess who claimed that her airline discriminated against her because she flaunted her voodoo equipment on the job. A young man fascinated by an expensive dress in a boutique window complained of discrimination because the shopkeeper would not let him try it on. The three suits were dismissed, but not before the various state enforcement agencies had held hearings.

Many civil rights advocates fear that a quota system could generate a backlash that would undo the progress of recent years. Throughout the seventies and into the eighties, a variety of public opinion polls indicated public support for affirmative action when it involved compensatory programs, such as additional job training for minorities, but overwhelming opposition to quotas. When the *New York Times* editorially endorsed the quota system that had kept Allan Bakke out of medical school, the letters in response ran at a 15 to 1 ratio against the paper's stand, and this from a predominantly liberal readership. A decade later, some observers believed they saw overt evidence of that backlash in the growing number of racial incidents on college campuses and the growth of racist skinhead groups. "Whether rightly or wrongly," wrote Gerald Kreyche, "the underlying mood of many white males is that they perceive themselves as bearing the brunt of so many of society's burdens that they don't want to take any more." As a sign of what they considered unfairness, six white police officers in

New York asked that their racial classification be changed to black or Hispanic so they could qualify for promotion under a racial quota system.

The counsel for the Senate Subcommittee on the Constitution has publicly worried that as affirmative action quotas became more institutionalized, the country officially would have to categorize its citizens by race. The Minority Business Enterprise program, in which Congress mandated that 10 percent of public works funds go to minority-owned firms, defined such companies as those owned by "Negroes, Spanish-speaking, Orientals, Indians, Eskimos and Aleuts."

That quotas could lead to such classification is certainly one of the complaints that Jewish groups, long allies of blacks in the civil rights struggle, have raised and that has put such a strain on that alliance. Jews remember that in Europe the infamous *numerus clausus* kept them out of universities and the professions and that even in the United States, many colleges and medical schools had Jewish quotas that crippled rather than helped bright young men and women. Morris Abrams, head of the American Jewish Committee, charged that quotas create an "ethnic spoils system," that pits one group against another and that will inevitably result in an "institutionalized division of the pie of opportunity by bureaucratic decisions as to the group disadvantaged and the numbers of each group to be benefited." In a passionate and moving essay, legal scholar Alexander Bickel argues,

> A racial quota derogates the human dignity and individuality of all to whom it is applied; it is invidious in principle as well as in practice. Moreover, it can easily be turned against those it purports to help. The history of the racial quota is a history of subjugation, not beneficence. Its evil lies not in its name, but in its effects; a quota is a divider of society, a creator of castes, and it is all the worse for its racial base, especially in a society desperately striving for an equality that will make race irrelevant.

As for past injustices, most critics of affirmative action do not deny that blacks, women, and other groups have been discriminated against but maintain that it is illogical and unfair to compensate present members of these groups for ills suffered by their ancestors, at the expense of other, and innocent, groups today. It simply does not follow, charged Carl Cohen, either "in morals or in law, that individual blacks, or orientals, or Jews, who were not damaged are entitled now to special favor in the name of group redress." In a blunter tone, EEOC Commissioner Fred Alvarez declared, "When somebody tells me they ought to get something because they're Irish and saw signs in Boston that said IRISH NEED NOT APPLY . . . or because their ancestors were in slavery, I say 'So what?' "

Another fear, especially among educators, is that colleges and universities will be forced to accept unqualified students, and in order to do so, will have to lower their overall standards. In California, for example, a state report noted that only 3.6 percent of the state's black public high school graduates and 4.9 percent of the Hispanic graduates would have been eligible under regular admission standards to the elite University of California Berkeley campus, compared to 13.2 percent of all graduating seniors. As a result, more than half of the black first-time freshmen and almost that high a ratio of Hispanics were "special admissions" students. To gain admission, applicants in targeted "protected" classes had to graduate from high school with a GPA of at least 3.3 *or* earn a GPA of 2.79–3.29 and have sufficiently high test scores *or* score at least 1,100 on the College Board's Scholastic Aptitude Tests (SATs). In contrast, white or Asian students needed a GPA of 3.7 or better for admission. The result, as Andrew Hacker notes, is that although the Berkeley and UCLA campuses, the showpieces of the California system, have a more diverse student body, the schools do not necessarily have as well-qualified a group of students.

In a society where education is perhaps the key to economic and social mobility, access to educational opportunity is obviously crucial for minorities. Yet the very groups that have sought such access have also been the least prepared; it is not a question of blacks being intellectually inferior. They and other minorities have suffered from poor schooling, a legacy of society's pervasive discrimination against them. When some public college systems instituted an open admissions policy, blacks poured into those schools, and in many instances, failed out almost as quickly, while driving away faculty and qualified white students. Even when colleges did provide remedial services, many minority students rejected this help as patronizing.

Even in the elite schools, as Thomas Sowell charges, "the drive to get a good-looking 'body count' of black students leads the top colleges and universities to go way beyond the pool of black students to meet their normal admission standards." This effort may ease the conscience of white administrators, but unfortunately "many black students discover too late that the 'opportunity' to go to a big-name school turns out to be a trap."

The larger question to some educators, however, is whether colleges and universities are the appropriate agencies to undertake the task of remedying decades of social discrimination. The purpose of a university is to advance knowledge and to benefit society by training the best and brightest of the new generation in the arts, humanities, sciences, and the professions. Advocates of affirmative action argue that maintaining high academic standards will mean too few educated minority members, which will hurt the country in the long run. But so, too, will the failure to educate the nation's very brightest if resources are diverted to compensatory programs. The university, John Bunzel reminds us, "is not the Department of Health and Human Services, and should not be mistaken as an adjunct agency of the federal government in the important business of political and social reform."

———

By the early 1980s, most large employers had adopted some form of affirmative action program; they had the staff and an employee pool large enough to manipulate in order to meet government requirements. Complaints increased, however, from small firms who tried to comply with federal regulations that, in their context, made no sense. Jim Supica, Jr., a building contractor in Lenexa, Kansas, claimed that federal rules had created a nightmare for his small bridge-building company. He employed fifteen men, three of them black, but the government cited the firm for not meeting the numerical goals of 12.7 percent minority-group members and 6.9 percent women in one job category, truck drivers. Supica, however, employs only two truck drivers, both white males who, as he pointed out, could sue him for reverse discrimination if he fired them to hire a black or a woman. Other small firms also complained about the inordinate amount of paperwork required by the government.

In his 1980 campaign for the presidency, Ronald Reagan constantly attacked the government for interfering too much in the private sector, and he also made it clear that he opposed employment quotas in any form. Shortly after the election, Sen. Orrin G. Hatch, scheduled to be chairman of the Senate Labor and Human Resources Committee, let it be known that his committee would pressure the Labor Department's Office of Federal Contract Compliance Programs to take a softer approach on affirmative action goals. If the OFCCP failed to take the hint, Hatch promised to introduce legislation forcing it to do so. The senator could count on help from one of the new president's closest advisers, Edwin Meese, who strongly opposed quotas.

In its first term, the Reagan administration sent mixed signals on affirmative action. In 1983, for example, Executive Order 12432 required federal agencies to increase their "goals" for employment of minority-owned subcontractors by at least 10 percent, at the same time that high officials in the government denounced all such "quotas" as illegal. Reagan reconstituted the U.S. Commission on Civil Rights, and the new majority firmly opposed any use of numerical quotas. At the same time, the Civil Rights Division of the Justice Department, led by William Bradford Reynolds, openly attacked affirmative action programs. Mary Frances Berry, a holdover member of the Civil Rights Commission, charged that the commission had "become a twin of the Civil Rights Division of the Justice Department, and the bank of justice, as Martin Luther King used to say, is now bankrupt. . . . I despair for women and minorities in this country." In response to some complaints from former staff members that the commission no longer accepted their reports, Morris Abram, the Reagan-appointed vice-chairman, responded that the facts put forward by the staff were irrelevant. "The decision to support or abhor racial tests for jobs in America should not be based on empirical data. Of course quotas work. They give jobs to those preferred and deny jobs to the victims of the new discrimination."

The attack on federal affirmative action programs took on a more strident tone in Reagan's second term, when Meese became attorney general. In his first press conference at the Justice Department, Meese approved affirmative action plans that sought to widen recruiting and training programs but expressed his implacable opposition to quotas. The Justice Department shortly thereafter sent out letters to fifty city governments that had signed consent decrees establishing hiring plans for women and minorities, informing them that it believed such plans unconstitutional. The strong reaction to this policy seemed to indicate that both public and private sector officials stood diametrically opposed to the administration's policy.

The National Association of Manufacturers Equal Employment Opportunity Committee, alerted to Meese's plan, opposed any proposal that would weaken federal requirements and passed a ringing endorsement of affirmative action as a national social policy. In Omaha, Los Angeles, Cincinnati, and elsewhere, city officials declared that they would not back away from a program that had proven successful. As John Myers, deputy solicitor for Philadelphia, explained, "It was the right thing to do when we entered into the decree, and it's still the right thing to do." Although Meese kept up his attack on any plans that included hiring goals, the public uproar alerted Reagan's more astute political advisers to leave the issue alone. Labor Secretary William Brock publicly defended affirmative action and his department's enforcement of federal policy, and managed to block Meese's efforts to have Reagan repeal the executive orders establishing the program. When the president and the attorney general left office in January 1989, they left a legacy of eight years of indifference to civil rights, but the various federal regulations concerning affirmative action remained intact.

———

Not all the voices in the debate are strident; occasionally one finds a still, small voice of reason. Hyman Bookbinder of the American Jewish Committee reflected the concerns of many Jews over the growing split with the black community over affirmative action. The Jewish community, he declared, would continue to support a whole range of affirmative action goals, including the "prudent" use of goals and timetables, but would oppose "rigid, inflexible, preferential quotas." But the goals/quota debate, he asserted, diverted attention from other aspects of the fight for equal opportunity:

> If tomorrow morning, by some inexplicable miracle, every American citizen and every American company or institution were suddenly entirely free of any prejudice and were determined forever to end discrimination, it would take a long time before our labor

force would reflect the mix of our general population. Too many would remain unprepared for the new opportunities.

It is equally true that if tomorrow morning, by some inexplicable miracle, every American sub-group — blacks, Hispanics, women, etc. — had the same range of qualified individuals for the whole range of employment opportunities, it would similarly take a long time before our labor force would reflect the mix of our general population. Too many Americans and American institutions, unfortunately, would still be unprepared to abandon their prejudices and habits.

The struggle for equal opportunity has to be pursued in both arenas, eradicating prejudice on the one hand and providing better education and job training on the other. Too great a concern with institutional prejudice, leading to quotas, he concluded, has diverted the nation from dealing with the goals of creating more opportunity for its citizens.

The debate over affirmative action, while too often generating more heat than light, has nonetheless forced Americans to ask some hard questions. Admitting that women, blacks, and other minorities suffered and still suffer discrimination at the hands of a white male-dominated society, what is fair? Should the government impose a policy that benefits women and minorities at the expense of white males? Is race-conscious and gender-conscious affirmative action the proper policy to achieve a truly race-blind and gender-blind society? Can women and minorities ever achieve true equal opportunity in education and employment without such programs? Does affirmative action work to benefit large numbers of women and minorities, or does it help only the few who would succeed in any event? Is a practice that discriminates against one group, even to compensate victims of past discrimination, the right policy for a democratic society pledged to the equal protection of the laws for all its citizens?

Such questions are at the heart of the debate, and as Alexis de Tocqueville noted long ago, in the United States all public issues eventually become legal questions. Even as political leaders tried to define what affirmative action meant, the courts pondered whether and how the Constitution allowed such programs.

CHAPTER 3

The Law and Affirmative Action

As Judge Ingram prepared to hear Paul Johnson's suit, he had a certain body of legal precedent to guide him. The Supreme Court by spring 1982 had decided several cases dealing with affirmative action and had also considered questions regarding discrimination against women. It had not, as yet, heard any cases directly involving women and affirmative action, but these two paths of law had converged in some areas. In general, the law as expounded by the high court condemned discrimination in employment based on immutable characteristics such as race or gender and approved, albeit sometimes guardedly, efforts to remedy the effects of past discrimination. But just as affirmative action had proved socially divisive, it also caused deep splits on the bench.

In the 1960s and 1970s, Congress passed a number of measures designed to attack racial discrimination in general, and in employment in particular. The most notable of these measures remains Title VII of the 1964 Civil Rights Act, but in the following years Congress passed several other measures aimed at eliminating discrimination in employment. In the Equal Employment Opportunity Act of 1972, Congress statutorily confirmed several lower court decisions that had interpreted Title VII to mean that affirmative steps could be taken by the courts to remedy discrimination. The 1972 law also expanded the coverage of Title VII by including state and local government employees, as well as those in federal executive agencies, in its protection.

In the next few years Congress addressed other forms of employment discrimination. Title IX of the Higher Education Act of 1972 forbade sex discrimination in educational institutions receiving federal funds. The Vocational Rehabilitation Act of 1973 required federal contractors to provide employment opportunities for disabled and other veterans of the Vietnam War. The Age Discrimination Act of 1975, as well as several State and Local Fiscal Assistance Acts, spread the umbrella of congressional protection even further, taking in rage, gender, religion, age, and disability. Moreover, by 1982 most of the fifty states also had some form of antidiscrimination statutes, some of which went even further than federal law in covering such categories as prior arrest records or marital status. A number of municipalities also passed local ordinances targeted at specific types of discrimination.

With these laws on federal, state, and local statute books, case law began to expand. The Supreme Court had heard cases involving employment discrimination as early as World War II and had tentatively started to limn out a legal notion of fair employment. In a 1944 case, *Steele v. Louisville & Nashville Railroad Co.*, it had ruled that trade unions governed by the Railway Labor Act owed black and other minority union members a duty to represent them "without hostile discrimination, fairly, impartially, and in good faith." The case had limited applicability because it affected only those unions operating under federal law. Otherwise, discrimination in the private job market did not then seem amenable to court remedy.

Between 1948 and 1961, however, the Court decided a number of civil rights cases that cast doubt on the previous immunity of private discrimination against the reach of the equal protection clause. It struck down judicial enforcement of racially based restrictive covenants, and following the school desegregation cases, determined that when governmental activity intertwined with private discrimination, then the latter constituted a form of state activity proscribed by the Fourteenth Amendment.

Despite all the civil rights cases it had decided up to 1965, the Court had not really established any firm doctrinal guidelines by which to evaluate the problems that Title VII would generate. The law itself spoke more to broad objectives than to specifics. For example, while it prohibited employment discrimination, it did not define what constituted proof of that discrimination. Beyond the obvious, such as "whites only" or "men only," what constituted a discriminatory practice? Did the law reach the effects of past practices, even if those practices had been abolished prior to the new law? What did the law intend if an existing, and bona fide, seniority system encouraged some discriminatory practices? What conduct sufficed to show "intentional" discrimination? What if employment tests tended to disfavor certain groups? Above all, what remedies could the courts order if they found discrimination? According to Robert Belton, the courts faced these issues in three "generations" of cases. The first involved procedural issues, such as whether a plaintiff could sue in federal court before going to the EEOC; the second generation centered on definitions of what constituted unlawful discrimination; and the third dealt with appropriate judicial remedies.

Though it is beyond the scope of this book to trace the entire judicial development of Title VII and employment discrimination, a few cases need to be discussed because their rulings would affect the progress of Paul Johnson's suit as it made its way through the courts.

One of the earliest cases, *Griggs v. Duke Power Company* (1971), involved the question of how one determined if, in fact, discrimination existed. The Duke Power Company required new applicants for jobs as well as those employees seeking transfer or promotion to have a high school diploma and to take a standardized general intelligence test. Given the inferior education that most blacks had received in North Carolina, the tests tended to keep them confined to the least skilled and lowest paid ranks within the company. Several blacks filed a class action suit charging that the tests had no relevance to job skills and, in fact, existed solely to perpetuate job segregation within the company.

In speaking for an 8-to-0 Court, Chief Justice Warren Burger found that the tests, while neutral on their face (that is, the same tests were administered to both black and white applicants), nonetheless had a "disparate impact" in that they resulted in job discrimination. Congress had intended, Burger said, to prohibit not only overt discrimination but also those practices that perpetuated discrimination. "If an employment practice which operates to exclude Negroes cannot be shown to be related to job performance, the practice is prohibited." Legitimate tests that related to job skills would be permitted under Title VII, but the employer had to establish that relationship. In *Washington v. Davis* (1976), the Court did sustain tests administered by the District of Columbia Police Department, even though these tests tended to screen out more black than white applicants. The Police Department proved that the skills measured by the tests had a direct relationship to the skills it required of its police officers.

Aside from the question of testing, the *Griggs* case provided civil rights advocates with what seemed a sure-fire tool to prove the existence of job discrimination, the disparate impact theory. Plaintiffs could establish the discriminatory nature of a particular practice, such as an irrelevant test, by statistics demonstrating that a racial imbalance resulted from that practice. In a 1977 case, Justice Potter Stewart declared that statistics by themselves could prove the existence of employment discrimination. Moreover, they did not have to prove that the employer had a discriminatory motive; only that the practice, whatever the reason, discriminated against blacks or other minorities. Disparate impact analysis also gave employers, such as Santa Clara County, indications of where problems might be in their work force, so they could design programs to address those imbalances.

Employers, however, could often identify a problem far more easily than they could design remedies, since a number of conditions affected the employment profile. A high-tech firm, for example, would need well-educated workers, and past patterns of segregated and inferior schooling may have resulted in very few blacks having the necessary background. A firm located in a university town in the 1960s could often count upon a pool of graduate-student wives, themselves highly educated but willing to work for very low wages out of economic necessity, and as a result distorting the employment picture. How much did cultural patterns, status considerations, availability of transportation, a seniority system, a union contract — none of which specifically intended to discriminate — affect employment patterns in a prejudicial manner? To overcome these and other conditions, as well as to remedy the effects of past discrimination, executive orders and congressional statutes called for affirmative action, a concept noble in purpose but fraught with legal problems.

Early cases involving affirmative action rose under the various executive orders promulgated by presidents Kennedy, Johnson, and Nixon. In *Farmer v. Philadelphia Electric Co.* (1963), the first case of record under the 1961 executive order, a federal district court sidestepped the entire question of discrimination by ruling that the plaintiff could not sue, since he had not availed himself of the administrative procedures established by the executive order. Other early cases also tended to focus on procedural technicalities rather than on constitutional issues. The Supreme Court, no doubt aware of the legal landmines in affirmative action, tried to evade the issue as long as possible, and denied certiorari in several appeals of these early decisions. Eventually, however, the high court had to confront the legal and constitutional questions raised by affirmative action, and it chose to begin this examination not in the context of employment programs but in preferential admissions plans for schools.

In the various desegregation cases following *Brown*, the Court had ruled that any racial classification faced strict scrutiny — the highest level of judicial review. Nonetheless, the Court confirmed a number of race-conscious voluntary school integration plans without imposing strict scrutiny, supposedly because these plans helped blacks instead of discriminating against them.

A number of colleges and graduate schools, sensitive to the fact that conscious or unconscious policies had previously barred minorities from higher education, instituted preferential admissions programs, often without any specific findings that they themselves had discriminated. White students, denied admissions for allegedly less qualified blacks, launched a number of Title VII challenges against these programs in the early 1970s. In the first case to reach the Supreme Court, a bare majority of the justices chose to avoid the issue.

Marco DeFunis challenged a preferential admissions program at the University of Washington Law School on the grounds that he had been denied admission in favor of a less qualified black. While the case was in litigation, the university allowed DeFunis to attend the law school, and by the time it reached the Supreme Court, he was about to graduate. As a result, five of the justices joined in a *per curiam* decision dismissing the suit as moot. Of the four who voted against the dismissal, only William O. Douglas wrote an opinion that actually dealt with the merits of the case, and the man who arguably may have been the most liberal justice to sit on the Court in this century strongly condemned racial considerations in admissions programs, even for benign purposes:

{ *Affirmative Action on Trial* }

A DeFunis who is white is entitled to no advantage by virtue of that fact; nor is he subject to any disability, no matter what his race or color. Whatever his race, he had a constitutional right to have his application considered on its individual merits in a racially neutral manner.

The Court had sidestepped the issue temporarily, but it would not go away. In *DeFunis v. Odegaard* "the bomb failed to go off"; four years later it exploded in *Regents of the University of California v. Bakke* (1978), next to abortion the most controversial decision of the 1970s. Allan Bakke, a thirty-seven-year-old white male, had been denied admission to the University of California Medical School at Davis. He contended that the school's special admissions program, which reserved sixteen slots in a class of one hundred for disadvantaged minority students, operated to deprive him of his rights under the California constitution, Title VI of the 1964 Civil Rights Act, and the Equal Protection Clause of the Fourteenth Amendment. Unlike De-Funis, Bakke had not been allowed to register, and so the Court could not hide behind a mootness issue. Did a program that consciously favored minorities and as a result discriminated against whites, whether in education or in employment, violate federal law and the Constitution? Specifically, the Court had to answer two questions. Could race be a legitimate factor in admissions decisions (and by implication in other public and private programs)? If so, did this particular program operate in a way to violate either Title VII or the Equal Protection Clause?

Civil rights advocates as well as opponents of affirmative action watched the progress of the *Bakke* case carefully. Benjamin Hooks of the NAACP warned that if the Court ruled in favor of Bakke, "everything that has happened in the last twenty years will be rolled back." Conservative John H. Bunzel hoped the Court would find for Bakke, because affirmative action undermined basic premises of American society. "In a country of many minority groups," he asked, "is it possible to discriminate in favor of a minority without discriminating against another minority (let alone the majority)?" Few people approached the level of hysteria that McGeorge Bundy did in warning that if the Court did not support the Davis plan, it would be turning its back on blacks and others seeking to escape the legacy of discrimination. The *Bakke* case, he declared, has "an importance not exceeded by any single case from the past, not the *Brown* case of 1954, and not the *Dartmouth College* case itself, in which the independence of the chartered private college was first upheld."

The nine justices filed six separate opinions, with no majority agreeing on any one point. Four of the justices — William Brennan, Byron White, Thurgood Marshall, and Harry Blackmun — believed that neither the Civil Rights Act nor the Fourteenth Amendment invalidated affirmative action programs, and therefore Bakke should not be admitted. Four others — Burger, Stewart, William Rehnquist, and John Paul Stevens — adopted a straightforward statutory interpretation: the law said no racial discrimination, the Davis program had excluded Bakke because of his race, and he should be admitted.

Lewis Powell attempted to break the deadlock in an opinion that received full endorsement from none of his brethren. In his opinion he ruled that race could be a factor in admissions programs (the Brennan group supported him on this point), but that the Davis program had used race incorrectly, thus discriminating against Bakke, who should now be admitted (the Burger group joined this part of the opinion).

Powell had evidently struck this balance early in the Court's deliberations but had been unable to win over any of his colleagues, a sign, if any were needed after *DeFunis*, that affirmative action would be a divisive issue within the Court. The decision would be widely attacked by both proponents and opponents of affirmative action, but whatever its legal merits, it seemed an astute political compromise, designed to buy time in which the Court could sort out some of the troubling issues raised by affirmative action.

Meg Greenfield, writing in *Newsweek*, had in fact predicted that the Court would find a way to "blur the edges of the controversy" while at the same time reaffirming the important values on both sides of the question. "You say that is fudging the issue?" she asked. "Fine. It ought to be fudged." That approach would allow employers to continue to work on solutions to the problems caused by past discrimination, but with greater care that the solution related directly to problems it had caused. One of the defects in the Davis program had been that the relatively new medical school did not have a record of discrimination against blacks and other minorities but had undertaken to address a larger social problem. Affirmative action plans could continue, but the *Bakke* decision left many questions in the air that the Court would have to address in the near future.

The Court answered at least some of these questions fairly quickly. In the very next term, it examined an affirmative action plan voluntarily adopted by a private employer, and its decision in *United Steelworkers of America v. Weber* (1979) would be its definitive statement for the next several years. In 1974 the United Steelworkers and the Kaiser Aluminum and Chemical Company signed a collective bargaining agreement that included an affirmative action plan. At the time, practically no blacks held the higher paying skilled-crafts positions, and the union and the company agreed that Kaiser would establish an in-plant training program and reserve 50 percent of the slots in these programs for blacks. The goal would be for blacks eventually to hold a percentage of the skilled-crafts positions equivalent to the percentage of blacks in the local labor force. One of the criteria for selection into the training programs would be seniority in the plant.

At the Kaiser plant in Gramercy, Louisiana, management set up a training program that accepted thirteen people, seven black and six white. The most senior black worker chosen had less seniority than several white workers who had not been accepted. One of them, Brian Weber, filed a class action suit charging discrimination under Title VII. Both the district court and the Court of Appeals for the Fifth Circuit ruled that the plan violated the Civil Rights Act in that it granted preference based solely on race.

The Supreme Court, speaking through Justice Brennan in a 5-to-2 decision, reversed the lower courts and ruled that Title VII did not prohibit race-conscious affirmative action plans. Brennan, probably in order to sustain his majority, emphasized the narrowness of the decision. The Kaiser plan did not involve either the state or the federal government and thus did not trigger any constitutional considerations.* The only question the Court would answer, then, was

---

* The Due Process and Equal Protection Clauses operate only against the state and federal governments and do not apply to private actors. To mount a constitutional claim, therefore, a governmental employer must be involved; if a private employer is charged with discrimination, the case must be brought under Title VII or another statute.

whether Title VII actually forbade "private employers and unions from voluntarily agreeing upon bona fide affirmative action plans." Title VII, of course, applied to whites as well as blacks, and its purpose had been to prevent any discrimination based on race.

A literal meaning of Title VII would prohibit any affirmative action plan, but an examination of the statutory history showed clearly that Congress had intended the law to deal with discrimination against Negroes and that it had not intended to foreclose voluntary programs to remedy the effects of past bias. In fact, the very wording of the statute, as well as statements in the accompanying House and Senate reports, supported the view that Congress wanted the bill to spur employers and unions to examine their own practices and to take voluntary steps not only to remove discriminatory practices but to work toward full equality. "It would be ironic indeed," Brennan noted,

> if a law triggered by a Nation's concern over centuries of racial injustice and intended to improve the lot of those who had "been excluded from the American dream for so long" (remarks of Sen. Humphrey), constituted the first legislative prohibition of all voluntary, private, race-conscious efforts to abolish traditional patterns of racial segregation and hierarchy.

But, Brennan concluded, Title VII did not automatically legitimate any plan merely because it claimed the title of affirmative action.

> The plan does not unnecessarily trammel the interests of the white employees. The plan does not require the discharge of white workers and their replacement with new black hires. Nor does the plan create an absolute bar to the advancement of white employees; half of those trained in the program will be white. Moreover, the plan is a temporary measure; it is not intended to maintain racial balance, but simply to eliminate a manifest racial imbalance. Preferential selection at the Gramercy plant will end as soon as the percentage of black skilled craftworkers in the Gramercy plant approximates the percentage of blacks in the local labor force.

Here we have what came to be the *Weber* criteria, the standards by which affirmative action plans would be judged for the next several years:

- The interests of whites would, to some extent, be restricted, but not to an unnecessary degree, and no white worker could be fired to make room for a black.
- The plan would have to be temporary, with either a fixed end date or a specific goal that would terminate the program.
- The plan could not be used to maintain a fixed percentage of minority workers, but only to eliminate obvious disparities.

The chief justice filed a relatively brief dissent that in essence said he would be glad to vote for such a plan if he were a member of Congress, a body charged with making public policy. The majority had, in his opinion, transgressed the line separating judicial from legislative responsibility, and in its interpretation of what Title VII meant had engaged in legislative amendment, distorting the original meaning of the words.

Justice Rehnquist proved far less restrained in his impassioned dissent, comparing the majority's reading of the plain words of Title VII to George Orwell's *Nineteen Eighty-Four*. The Court had been consistent, at least until this day, in holding that Title VII prohibited *all* racial discrimination in employment, and "were Congress to act today specifically to prohibit the type of racial discrimination suffered by Weber, it would be hard pressed to draft language better tailored to the task than that found in § 703(d) of Title VII." Now, like Orwell's characters, the majority said that the words meant exactly the opposite of what they had meant only a short time earlier.

The differences between the Brennan and Rehnquist opinions continued the split in *Bakke*, between the liberal wing of the Court, which believed race-conscious programs permissible to remedy past injustice, and the conservative bloc, which held that to achieve a society free of racial injustice, any and all discrimination based on race, be it directed against blacks or whites, had to be prohibited. Here the Court did no more than mirror the philosophical split in the larger society, and despite the fact that only two members of the Court dissented, only five of the justices — a bare majority — upheld the Kaiser plan. A shift of one or two votes, or one or two new appointees, and the Court might reverse *Weber*.

The very next term, an even more fractured Court upheld congressionally mandated set-aside programs. Affirmative action programs could take a variety of forms, such as preferential admissions to schools *(Bakke)* or job-training programs *(Weber)*. In 1977 Congress took notice of extensive discrimination against minority contractors in the construction industry, and in the Public Works Employment Act of that year, required that 10 percent of federal funds supplied for local public works projects had to be spent with businesses owned and controlled by members of identified minority groups.

The lead opinion in *Fullilove v. Klutznik* (1980) came from the chief justice, joined only by White and Powell. Burger noted that Congress had found extensive evidence of racial bias in the construction industry, and that sufficed as the predicate by which Congress could act under its remedial authority in Section 5 of the Fourteenth Amendment as well as its larger authority under the Commerce Clause. But if Congress had the power, had it chosen a legitimate means, namely the use of racial and ethnic criteria? Relying on various decisions in the school desegregation cases, Burger held that in appropriate circumstances, race-conscious remedies passed constitutional muster. Applying a variation of the *Weber* criteria, the chief justice reiterated the broad remedial power assigned to Congress and ruled that the set-aside program came within this power.

So stood employment law in terms of affirmative action as Paul Johnson made his way to the courthouse in spring 1982. But in addition to statutes and case law regarding racial discrimination, the 1970s had also seen the rise of the women's movement and corresponding efforts to modify the law as it affected women's rights in American society.

———

Prior to 1971, the Supreme Court passively accepted the general view of women as a group in need of legal protection, akin to children and the mentally retarded. Women confronted a legal and social system that for centuries had placed them in a position subordinate to men. They could not own property in their own name, could not vote, serve on juries, sue in tort or contract, and when married, found themselves totally at the mercy of their husbands. Marriage made man and woman into one, and that one, as far as the law was concerned, the man.

During the Progressive Era reformers attempted to ameliorate the condition of women workers by enacting protective legislation establishing maximum hours and minimum wages. Later feminists condemned these laws — supported at the time by both male and female reformers — as but another example of male domination, and no doubt they do reflect the predominant male view of women in need of special care. For the most part, jurists tended to view all gender-based classification as designed for women's benefit, protection, or both, and applied a simple rational basis test in the few instances when confronted with equal protection challenges.

The Supreme Court, for example, had no trouble sustaining state statutes that denied women the right to practice law, for as Justice Joseph Bradley wrote in *Bradwell v. Illinois* (1873):

> Man is, or should be, women's protector and defender. The natural and proper timidity which belongs to the female sex evidently unfits it for many of the occupations of civil life. The constitution of the family organization, which is founded in the divine ordinance, as well as in the nature of things, indicates the domestic sphere as that which properly belongs to the domain and functions of womanhood. The harmony, not to say identity, of interests and views which belong, or should belong, to the family institution is repugnant to the idea of a woman adopting a distinct and independent career from that of her husband. . . . The paramount destiny and mission of women are to fulfil the noble and benign offices of wife and mother. That is the law of the Creator.

In 1948, the Court upheld a Michigan law that prohibited a woman from obtaining a bartender's license unless "the wife or daughter of the male owner." Justice Felix Frankfurter, speaking for a 6-to-3 majority, declared that the Michigan legislature had acted rationally, and the Court would not second-guess its belief that "the oversight [of a woman's virtue] assured through ownership of a bar by a barmaid's husband or father minimizes hazards that may confront a barmaid without such protecting oversight."

For all that the Warren Court did in awakening America to the problems of racial discrimination, it did nothing regarding bias against women. As late as 1961, the Court upheld a Florida regulation preventing a woman voter's name from automatically being placed on a jury list, as would a man's; Justice Frankfurter found the state's assumption that a woman's place is in the home to be unexceptional.

Although some reformers have attempted to draw an analogy between legal discrimination faced by blacks and women, there is a difference. Professor, later Justice, Ruth Bader Ginsburg, who played a prominent role as advocate in a number of leading women's rights cases, pointed out that the generators of racial and sexual prejudice are not identical:

> Women are found in every neighborhood, in every economic class. They live in intimate association with men who, under traditional arrangements, held a control rein over them. Also of critical significance, the law's special treatment of women was long considered "preferential." Classification by sex was thought by gallant men to operate benignly in women's favor — to place women on a pedestal.

Interestingly, the allegedly conservative Burger Court began and sustained the legal revolution in women's rights. In *Reed v. Reed* (1971), a unanimous Court struck down an Idaho statute granting preference to men over women in the appointment of administrators of estates. The Court did not even begin to explore the ramifications of gender classification but applied a traditional equal protection analysis that emphasized procedural arbitrariness. Nonetheless, legal scholars as well as feminists believed that a new day had dawned and began to push the Court to declare gender a suspect classification, and one subject to the same strict scrutiny accorded racial classifications.

The Court came as close as it ever would two years later in *Frontiero v. Richardson* (1973), in which the justices struck down a federal law permitting male members of the armed forces automatically to receive a dependency allowance for their wives but requiring servicewomen to prove that they supported their husbands. Justice Brennan elaborated a powerful argument for treating gender as a suspect classification but won the support of only three other members of the Court — Douglas, White, and Marshall — one shy of the needed majority. Justice Powell, joined by Chief Justice Burger and Justice Blackmun, concurred in the result but refused to go as far as Brennan in declaring gender suspect. Only Justice Rehnquist dissented, on grounds that since sex was not a suspect classification, the law could be sustained on a rational basis test.

Over the next few years the Burger Court struck down several statutes that discriminated on the basis of sex, without achieving a consensus on the doctrine that justified such results. In *Craig v. Boren* (1976), however, the Court seemed to have found the rationale it had been seeking, a level of "intermediate scrutiny" more demanding than the simple rational basis test, yet not as stringent as the strict scrutiny applied to racial classifications. To withstand an equal protection challenge, Justice Brennan explained, "classification by gender must serve important governmental objectives and must be substantially related to achievement of those objectives." Henceforth intermediate scrutiny would be the standard by which any gender distinction, benign or invidious, would be judged.

One wonders why the Court never took the logical next step in developing a law that would ideally be as blind to gender as it would be toward race. The whole idea of equal protection is that the law applies to all persons in the same manner, that accidents of birth — such as race or gender — do not put a person at a disadvantage before the law. Title VII, the statutory basis for equal opportunity in employment, makes no distinction between race and gender, declaring it illegal to discriminate because of an individual's race, color, religion, sex, or national origin. It is true that the Fourteenth Amendment had originally been intended to prevent racial discrimination, but the wording of the equal protection clause says that no state shall "deny to any *person* within its jurisdiction the equal protection of the laws."

Would the fact that the Court viewed gender discrimination as somehow more acceptable, at least in its less virulent forms, mean that affirmative action plans designed to redress the effects of past discrimination against women would face a higher hurdle in the courts? Following *Bakke*, at least some commentators believed that would indeed be the case. Racial discrimination law had always been the paradigm for all discrimination law, but the courts had rarely had any trouble in defining racial discrimination. Moreover, racial classification had been assumed, at least since World War II, to be malign and discriminatory; gender classification, on the other hand, had been assumed, at least until the 1970s, to be benign, and thus male judges often had difficulty in defining gender discrimination.

If the Court, which had been dealing with racial discrimination for more than thirty years, had so much difficulty with affirmative action based on race, how would it be able, without comparable analytical tools, to deal with affirmative action for gender? Justice Powell had been able to define specific instances in which affirmative action would be an acceptable remedy for past racial discrimination — intentional discrimination, facially neutral rules that serve as a pretext for discrimination, and neutral rules that perpetuate past intentional discrimination. But, feminists asked, what about the type of discrimination women had faced resulting from cultural assumptions about gender differences and stereotypical attitudes about sex roles? Women rarely faced signs that said "No Women Need Apply" or "Males Only." They did not go to public schools segregated by gender or have to drink from separate water fountains. Rather, their opportunities had been subtly but nonetheless effectively restricted by what society considered "appropriate" for women. Under Powell's *Bakke* analysis, gender-conscious remedies to eliminate this kind of discrimination would be prohibited.

———

By the late seventies no one could question that the status of women before the law had changed, but how far it had changed remained debatable. The courts no longer blindly deferred to legislative enactments that assumed a woman's place should be in the home; at the same time, the courts had refused to make gender a suspect category akin to race. In some cases judges showed a remarkable sensitivity to the subtleties of gender discrimination; in others, the courts approved so-called "benign" programs that allegedly discriminated in favor of women. "The female of the species," Justice Stewart told a group of Harvard students, "has the best of both worlds. She can attack laws that unreasonably discriminate against her while preserving those that favor her."

The only problem seemed to be that not everyone agreed on what laws unreasonably discriminated against women and which ones worked to their benefit. One solution would be to treat all forms of gender discrimination as wrong, the same way one viewed racial bias,

{ *Affirmative Action on Trial* }

and subject supposedly benign programs, such as affirmative action, to the same set of factual predicates for women and blacks. A few cases decided toward the end of the decade hinted that even if the high court refused to adopt strict scrutiny in theory, the justices had erected fairly high walls to distinctions based on sex.

In 1978, the majority rejected statistical evidence that women on the whole lived longer than men as a justification for charging women higher premiums for a retirement system that paid equal benefits to men and women. Justice Stevens acknowledged "that as a class, women live longer than men," but Title VII barred discrimination against any *individual*, and "the basic policy of the statute requires that we focus on fairness to individuals rather than fairness to classes." Two years later, the Court struck down a Missouri statute that set up differing requirements for widows and widowers to claim death benefits under the state's workmen's compensation law. In his opinion for an 8-to-1 Court, Justice White reiterated that gender classifications had to serve important governmental objectives, a confirmation that, at the very least, the Court still adhered to the notion of intermediate scrutiny.

This, then, was the law Judge Ingram had to work with as he gaveled his court to order. The Equal Protection Clause as well as Title VII prohibited outright discrimination based simply on race or gender, even though, although not always, the classification operated in a benign manner. In regard to affirmative action, the decisions in *Bakke* and *Weber* indicated that if certain conditions had been met, both public and private employers could institute plans to remedy the effects of past discrimination. Aside from broad statements of policy, however, Judge Ingram really had very little case law on which to rely; Paul Johnson's suit would be one of many that would help shape employment discrimination law in the 1980s.

CHAPTER 4

"A Simple Title VII Case"

When Case No. 81-1218, "Paul E. Johnson, Plaintiff, vs. Transportation Agency, Santa Clara County, California, Defendant," opened in Judge William A. Ingram's courtroom on Friday morning, May 7, 1982, only Diane Joyce felt any apprehension about either the trial or its outcome. Johnson and his attorney, James Dawson, believed they had an open-and-shut case of discrimination under Title VII; the county, represented by its deputy counsel, Steven Woodside, felt equally confident that it had acted within its lawful discretion. But Diane Joyce, the cause of all this, worried that something would go wrong. In the weeks preceding the trial she had called the union's executive director, Michael Baratz, several times to tell him that she did not think the county was taking this case very seriously. Baratz tried to reassure her that there would be no problem. He considered Johnson's suit "bizarre and ridiculous" and seven years later still thought the whole thing "cut and dried. . . . According to the county procedures, she took a test, she qualified, they could pick anybody they want on the list, and they picked her."

But Baratz liked Diane Joyce and valued her work for the union, so he asked one of the stewards, Kristy Sermersheim, to see if Joyce had any reason to be worried, and if so, whether the union should intervene. Sermersheim called Ann Ravel, who had been assigned the responsibility of initial preparation of the county's defense. Ravel assured her that "there's no problem. They have such a stupid case they will never even go to trial."

Still, Sermersheim pointed out that the union stood ready to join in if necessary. "We are real worried about this."

"Kristy, they are such fools," Ravel responded. "In the deposition the boss has said 'I hate Diane Joyce, and I hate women stewards.' You don't have to worry. This will never go to trial."

Sermersheim reported this conversation to her boss, Michael Baratz, and also called Diane Joyce to reassure her, to tell her that "Ann Ravel says this is easy and there will be no problem." So the union relaxed, and neither Baratz nor Sermersheim were aware that the case had gone to trial.

In fact, no one on the county's side seemed to worry. Suzanne Wilson, a member of the Board of Supervisors, recalled that Selby Brown, Jr., the county counsel, had informed the board of the suit, but the members saw it as a routine matter, "a low level case," nothing to get very concerned about. In the county's legal department, nothing about the case seemed to warrant special concern. After a briefing on the facts, Brown had decided to leave the matter in the hands of two of his deputies, Steven Woodside and Ann Ravel, both of whom had had previous experience with employment discrimination cases, including a few that went on appeal to the Ninth Circuit.

———

Only a handful of the tens of thousands of lawsuits decided in America each year wind up as cases before the Supreme Court, and even those later recognized as landmark decisions hardly ever appear as such at the trial stage. Yet looking back, there appears to have been an unusually relaxed atmosphere among the attorneys preparing this case. The county engaged in practically no discovery but relied almost entirely on the argument that under acceptable personnel procedures, the hiring official could choose any of the seven candidates who qualified for the position; if the affirmative action plan tipped the balance in favor of Diane Joyce, that did not violate any principle of law.

Jim Dawson thought he had a straight summary judgment under Title VII and the ruling in the *Weber* decision.* The county had discriminated against his client on the basis of gender, prohibited by Title VII, and the affirmative action plan did not meet, at least in his eyes, the criteria set forth in *Weber.* He did a little pretrial discovery, to

---

*When the law is clear and there is no dispute over the facts, a party may propose that the evidence so plainly supports its side that the judge should render a decision in its favor without the need for further argument or sending the case to the fact finder.

make sure that the facts as Johnson had reported them could be verified. His major decision had already been taken, in whether to go the state or the federal route.

In terms of employment law, the California code at that time had even stronger prohibitions against discrimination than did federal law, and since the parties involved were California residents or entities, he could have lodged his initial complaint with the California Department of Fair Employment and Housing. Dawson went to the Equal Opportunity Employment Commission because he considered the federal agency better equipped to handle complaints and because Paul Johnson wanted a fairly rapid determination, which he got. Once they had the EEOC right-to-sue letter in March 1981, they still could have gone into either state or federal court. At that time state and federal courts in California shared concurrent jurisdiction. State courts could determine suits either on state or federal theories of law, and the federal courts could do the same. The decisive factor was time, and with a backlog of cases causing extensive delays in state courts, Dawson had decided to file his suit in federal court.

Other lawyers later criticized Dawson for relying solely on statutory law and not invoking the constitutional argument of equal protection. Dawson admits that with twenty-twenty hindsight, he probably should have invoked equal protection, but at the time "I thought we had a slam-dunker under *Weber*, which is Title VII." Moreover, his prior experience with employment discrimination cases led him to believe that most judges looked at Title VII in much the same way but had widely disparate views on how constitutional equal protection theory applied in the job market. Constance Brooks, who later argued Johnson's case before the Supreme Court, defended Dawson's decision as absolutely proper lawyering. A lawyer's job is to win the client's case in the fastest, cheapest way possible, not to develop elaborate constitutional theories. Steve Woodside agreed. "He didn't think, and I certainly didn't think, that it was going to go anywhere beyond [the trial stage]. Maybe an appeal, but you don't sit there thinking this case is going to go to the Supreme Court and raise every issue to cover yourself."

Moreover, Paul Johnson did not want anything more than to have the court give him the job he believed he had earned fair and square. As a result, Dawson framed his strategy on an individual basis, not as

{ *Affirmative Action on Trial* }

an attack on affirmative action. We wanted to say, he explained, that affirmative action is all well and good, "but you have to use some care and precision when you're applying it, and that did not happen here. This was a back door job with someone who had some power with the county." Had his client wanted to launch a full frontal assault on affirmative action, Dawson would have employed different tactics. "We would have filed a constitutional claim, we would have filed state statutory claims of various types, and I suspect we would have associated someone else who could have carried the brunt of that additional cost." Instead, Dawson had what he considered a much simpler burden to bear — show that the county's affirmative action plan as it had applied to his client violated the 1964 Civil Rights Act prohibition against discrimination.

Because both sides believed that the law and the facts clearly supported their positions, they waived a jury trial and chose to have the judge decide the merits. Both Dawson and Woodside thought highly of William A. Ingram, whom they described as a gentleman and as a judge who knew the law and presided over trials fairly but firmly. The fifty-eight-year-old Ingram had moved to San Francisco from Kentucky after graduating from law school, and then a few years later moved south to San Jose. He had been a deputy district attorney and then a successful lawyer before going on to the California Superior Court in 1971. Woodside had, in fact, upon graduation from law school clerked for Ingram in the state court and had nothing but praise for him. In the 1970s the bar conducted an annual poll on judges, and local attorneys had consistently ranked Ingram number one in terms of fairness and ability.

President Ford had named Ingram to the federal bench in 1976, and once there, he lobbied for several years to get a division of the Northern District located in San Jose, so local lawyers, litigants, and witnesses would not have to make the trek to San Francisco. He ultimately secured a separate court for Santa Clara and three neighboring counties, and at the time of Paul Johnson's suit, construction had begun on a new federal court building. In the meantime, Judge Ingram heard cases in a temporary courtroom in a trailer.

Dawson also lauded Ingram as fair; "He is probably not a result-oriented liberal judge by anyone's stretch of the imagination." Dawson had earlier tried two Title VII cases before Ingram, and even though he had lost both of them, believed the judge had acted fairly. In the case of Paul Johnson, Dawson believed Ingram would look at the facts and apply the law fairly. Both sides, then, felt secure in their cases and content with the judge who would hear their pleas when the clerk called the court to order and asked opposing counsel to identify themselves.

———

After Judge Ingram gaveled the court to order, the plaintiff's attorney, James Dawson, opened the proceedings with a straightforward statement of his client's case — that Paul Johnson had been denied a promotion he had earned solely on the basis of gender, a violation of Title VII of the Civil Rights Act. Johnson "does not challenge the existence of the affirmative action plan, this one in particular, or affirmative action plans in general, but simply challenges the way [this plan] was used in this context." For sex or race or national origin to be used as an employment or promotion criterion, Dawson argued, "it has to be a remedial action, it has to be based on something other than general societal discrimination." The county did not have such a record of discrimination, and could support a claim only by categorizing the road dispatcher's job as a skilled-craft position. In fact, road dispatching required only clerical ability, and women already held 75 percent of the department's clerical and office positions.

Dawson took about ten minutes to sketch out his case, and when he had finished, the judge asked him what relief his client wanted.

"The plaintiff, your honor, requests that he be appointed to the position of road dispatcher retroactively to June of 1980, that he be afforded differential in pay between his present position and that of road dispatcher, that the court issue an injunction stating that the plaintiff will not be discriminated against again in connection with his sex. Plaintiff [also] requests costs of suit and reasonable attorney's fees."

Steven Woodside then presented the county's defense, namely that Paul Johnson was not better qualified than Diane Joyce, and unless he could prove that he had been passed over for someone of lesser qualification, he had not borne the burden of proof required for a Title VII discrimination case. The facts showed that both Joyce and Johnson had about the same qualifications and that the hiring supervisor had discretion to choose from among those who qualified in the top pool. Under the county's affirmative action plan, the fact that not a single woman held any of the road department's 238 skilled-craft jobs constituted a legitimate consideration in the eyes of the hiring authority.

Woodside recognized that he could not simply say that the county had adopted an affirmative action plan because it had deliberately discriminated against women and minorities in the past, since that would open the country to all sorts of Title VII lawsuits. Previous decisions in the Supreme Court had recognized this dilemma and had held that an employer did not have to admit to prior discrimination in order to implement an affirmative action plan. Woodside did admit that the county was in "a very vulnerable position in terms of Title VII, as a matter of defending history, given the very few women who have ever held a position of responsibility in road maintenance."

The county felt it had a much stronger case in regard to the question of whether the road dispatcher should be classified as a skilled or a clerical position. Because it had been classified as skilled long before the case arose, there could be no charge that the county had manipulated the classification for affirmative action purposes, and the numerical disparity — one woman out of 238 — seemed to support the county's claim. But Woodside had a fallback strategy. The plaintiff would have the burden of proving that the dispatcher's job had been misclassified, and if he could, if Dawson could show that it ought to be considered as clerical, then the county would argue that as a clerical worker, Diane Joyce had far better qualifications than Paul Johnson.

With the brief opening statements complete, Dawson called his first witness, James H. Graebner, director of the Transportation Agency, and the man who had chosen Diane Joyce over Paul Johnson. From later reports, it appears that Dawson had not intended Graebner to go first, that he planned to use his other witnesses to show that Johnson had the better qualifications and then had been passed over solely on the grounds of gender discrimination. But Graebner was getting married that weekend and did not want to delay his honeymoon if the trial ran more than one day, so he asked if he could testify first. Dawson agreed, but Woodside thus did not have a chance to go over Graebner's testimony with him and alert him to potential traps. As it turned out, Graebner's version of what happened seemed to support every one of Paul Johnson's assertions.

The Transportation Agency director acknowledged that he normally would not have been involved in the hiring process for a job at this level; that the road operations people wanted Paul Johnson; and that the affirmative action director, Victor Morton, had come to him to urge the appointment of the woman candidate.

Q. Mr. Morton felt that Diane Joyce should be appointed?

A. Mr. Morton was less interested in the particular individual; he felt that this was an opportunity for us to take a step toward meeting our affirmative action goals, and because there was only one person on the list who was one of the protected groups, he felt that this afforded us an opportunity to meet those goals through the appointment of that member of a protected group.

This brought Dawson almost immediately to the questions that he most wanted to ask.

Q. Mr. Graebner, did you have any basis to distinguish as whether or not one or the other was more qualified than the other?

A. No. They both appeared, and my conversations with people tended to corroborate, that they were both capable of performing the work.

Q. Did you take Ms. Joyce's sex into account in making the decision?

A. Yes.

Q. Was that a positive factor for Ms. Joyce?

A. In terms of affirmative action, yes.

Q. If Diane Joyce had not been on the eligible list, in your mind, would Mr. Johnson had been appointed?

A. Quite possibly. I see no reason why he wouldn't have been.

Dawson later noted that he thought Graebner "hadn't looked at this stuff in years," and for much of his examination, Dawson had to prompt the witness on how the agency's personnel policies and affirmative action plan worked. He spent a long time, unsuccessfully, trying to get the director to concede that the dispatcher's position did not require extensive skills and should, in fact, have been classified as a clerical position.

He had more luck in getting Graebner to concede that the county's affirmative action plan left an enormous amount of discretion to the hiring authority and that no clear guidelines existed as to how much race or gender should be taken into account when hiring or promoting people.

On his cross-examination of the witness, Steven Woodside tried to undo some of the damage, and he asked Graebner a number of questions to elicit statements that he had sufficient information that Joyce was as well qualified as Johnson for the job. Graebner, while certainly trying to be helpful, just did not know a lot about her other than she appeared to have performed her previous job duties satisfactorily. She had been chosen, quite clearly, because the affirmative action officer had said they should appoint a woman. Realizing that further testimony might prove even more damaging, Woodside cut it short.

Reflecting on the case, Woodside agreed that Graebner's evidence had been critical. An administrator more experienced with affirmative action and the problems it can generate might have privately decided to hire a person because of gender or race but publicly would have said, "I think she's well qualified for the job, and I've considered the other candidates, and my decision is Diane Joyce. Period." But Norman Graebner normally would not have even been involved with appointments at this level, and when confronted by Paul Johnson, "he owns up to his thought process and tells him absolutely honestly" why he had chosen Joyce. And, Woodside noted, Judge Ingram believed him, and questioned why gender should have been considered at all.

Following Graebner, Dawson called Diane Joyce to the stand and identified her as "the individual who was appointed to the position of road dispatcher." When asked if she thought herself more qualified than Paul Johnson at the time of the appointment, she looked Dawson in the eye and said, simply, "Yes."

Dawson carefully led Joyce through a recitation of her work experience in the highway agency and the type of skills one needed for dispatcher, trying to demonstrate that the job did not require any skills beyond clerical ability. In the middle of her testimony, Judge

Ingram decided that he had heard enough for the morning and recessed the trial at 12:30 for lunch. An hour later, Diane Joyce went
back on the stand to face more questions.

Dawson now switched tactics, to try to elicit from her why she
thought the process had been unfair, why she had decided to go to
affirmative action. He kept emphasizing that she had not scored as
highly as Paul Johnson on either of the two boards, but Diane Joyce
proved a cool witness.

> Q. When you walked into the second interview, Ms. Joyce, did you
> feel at that point that it was going to be unfair?
> A. Yes.
> Q. Was that because you were a woman?
> A. Yes.
> Q. Did you think the first oral interview was fair?
> A. Yes.
> Q. Do you think it was fair because there was a woman on the
> interview board?
> A. Yes.
> Q. Do you think it would have been less fair had there not been a
> woman on the interview board?
> A. Yes.
> Q. Why, in your opinion, did a woman being on the board make it
> more fair than if a woman hadn't been on the board?
> A. I believe it prevents collusion; keep[s] each other honest.
> Q. Simply because she's a woman.
> A. Yes.

Just as Woodside had recognized that further testimony from
Graebner would not help his case, so Dawson decided that he would
be better off getting Diane Joyce off the stand. Steven Woodside,
however, wanted to demonstrate something first. Where Dawson had
tried to show that she had not been as qualified as Paul Johnson,
Woodside now led her through a series of questions designed not
only to show that she had had extensive experience on the roads but
also to bring out some of the discrimination she had faced as the only
woman on the crews.

Diane Joyce gladly obliged him. She told the court how, when she
had first applied for a job with the transportation agency, the super-

visor had told her they wanted a man, but since no men had applied they would have to settle for a woman. She also told stories of how she had been singled out and reprimanded for actions that, if done by a man, would have gone unnoticed.

On reexamination, Dawson decided to follow up on these stories, on her active role as a union shop steward, and on the fact that she often filed complaints against the agency for actions she believed discriminatory.

> Q. How many grievances have you filed on your own behalf since you have been employed by the Transportation Agency?
> A. Regarding sex?
> Q. Regarding anything. Let's start with that.
> A. Five, ten.
> Q. How many of those have been resolved to your satisfaction?
> A. Ten.
> Q. They all have, is that correct?
> A. Yes.

Dawson did not push this line of questioning too far, since he did not want to depict Joyce as a victim. Rather, he wanted to show that because of her tendency to file complaints and her backing from the union, the county had promoted her over a more qualified applicant because it had been afraid she would sue if she did not get the job. To contrast to the "troublemaker," he next called his client, Paul Johnson, to the stand.

Johnson's suit alleged that he had been passed over for the promotion that he had earned because of his gender and that he was the victim of discrimination. Dawson wanted the court to see his client as a hardworking, decent man, one who had always played by the rules, and how the county had cheated him out of what he rightfully should have received — the dispatcher's post. Under Dawson's prompting, Johnson told his story, how he had worked hard in order to get the promotion, and then his amazement when Burt Di Basilio had told him that he had "already been appointed, and affirmative action got it reversed." He could not believe this, he told the court, and so he went through channels trying to get someone to explain what had happened. He had met with the affirmative action people, who told him they thought "it was a good opportunity to put a woman in the position." He had then met with the director, Mr. Graebner, who had told him essentially the same thing.

> Q. Mr. Johnson, did you feel that in May of 1980, at that time, that you were more qualified to do the job than Diane Joyce?
> A. No doubt in my mind.
> Q. What's the basis of your opinion?
> A. Well, first-off, performing the job, I guess, approximately ten months full-time, or fill-in time, plus possibly over approximately thirteen years, I probably worked as a dispatcher between two and a half and three years.
> Q. During the period of time that you functioned as a road dispatcher, did any of your superiors ever complain in connection with your job performance?
> A. None whatsoever.
> Q. Have you ever had any negative reviews in connection with your job performance with the county?
> A. No.
> Q. Have you ever had any counseling by a superior in connection with your job performance?
> A. None.
> Q. Have you ever filed a grievance against the county for anything?
> A. No.

When Dawson finished with his client, Steven Woodside made a somewhat half-hearted attempt to explore Johnson's past experience, to see if it could be made to compare unfavorably with that of Diane Joyce. But although Johnson had not had some of the experience she had had on the road crews, there could be no denying the fact that he had worked in the job and had done so quite satisfactorily. In a few minutes the county counsel decided that this further questioning would probably hurt his case more than help it, and he excused the witness. When Johnson stepped down from the stand, Judge Ingram recessed the court until 10:00 A.M. the following Wednesday.

———

In examining the testimony of that first day, the reader would be hard put to determine which side had an advantage, if any. James Graebner had testified that yes, he had chosen Diane Joyce for the simple fact that she was a woman, and he wanted to help meet affirmative action goals. Joyce had told about her experiences, and the discrimination she had faced, and how she had fought to overcome them, while Paul Johnson, in his own quiet way, had made a strong case that merit should be rewarded. If everyone seemed to agree on the key fact— that Johnson had been passed over so a woman could be appointed— this by itself did not necessarily violate the law. Affirmative action often means that white males who may not have personally been guilty of discriminatory activity will have to pay the costs of society's efforts to redress past injustice. Both Congress and the Supreme Court had said that under certain circumstances this would be acceptable as a matter of social policy. In his questioning, Dawson had tried to show that the circumstances of this case made a decision based solely on gender inappropriate; in response, Woodside had suggested that because Diane Joyce had been as well qualified as Paul Johnson, gender had been a legitimate consideration in light of the absence of women in the Transportation Agency's skilled-labor force. So far Judge Ingram had asked practically no questions, and neither side had any indication, at the end of that first day, of whether they were winning or losing.

When the trial resumed on May 12, Dawson intended to put four more witnesses on the stand, continuing his strategy of establishing that his client had been chosen because of his superior credentials and then had been deprived of the job by out-and-out discrimination. The county had only one witness, James Baldanzi, a road superintendent in the West Yard. Baldanzi felt sick that day, and Dawson agreed to let Woodside call him first, before continuing his own presentation.

Baldanzi had been a member of one of the interview panels, and in his testimony he indicated that he did not know a lot about Diane Joyce. Woodside, however, pressed his memory and brought out a deposition he had made in which Baldanzi had called Diane Joyce "a rebel-rousing, skirt-wearing person." Yes, he did recall that statement. Could he explain it? "Well," Baldanzi said, "Ms. Joyce was quite affiliated with the union that did not have full representation of the county in them days, and she more or less had the people going all different ways. I called it a rebel-rouser. This is my own personal opinion."

He denied, however, that he had let her union membership affect his judgment as a member of the panel; he had looked for someone with good experience for the dispatcher position.

Q. And who was that?

A. The gentleman that I came up with was Mr. Paul Johnson, I believe was the number one candidate.

Q. Is it correct to say that there were a number of candidates who were qualified to do the job?

A. I believe you could say that everybody was qualified or they wouldn't have been on the interview.

Although he had been unable to get Baldanzi to say outright that he would never have chosen Joyce over Johnson, Woodside had left the impression that Baldanzi and Johnson had been part of the old-boy network in the highway system, a network that would never have permitted a "rebel-rousing, skirt-wearing person" to breach their ranks.

On his cross-examination, Dawson tried to remove that impression and show that whatever his personal feelings, Baldanzi had been fair in his role as a member of the panel. Did he socialize with Paul Johnson? No. Did they work near each other? No, they worked in different facilities. How often did they see each other on the job? About once every four months. Did he ever discuss the dispatcher's opening with Paul Johnson? No. Did he ever discuss Ms. Joyce with the other two members of the panel outside of the interview? No, he had not. Had he had any preconceived ideas as to who should get the job? No, he had gone in with an open mind. Had the panel been unanimous in its selection of Mr. Johnson? Yes, it had.

An eager Steven Woodside began his redirect examination. He recalled Baldanzi's testimony that Diane Joyce's union activity had not influenced his judgment. But what about his deposition, in which he had said that her union activity conflicted with the requirements of road dispatcher, because "she manipulates people." Well, maybe he had said that, but he was not sure what he had meant at the time. Woodside pressed on.

Q. Did you also, in your deposition, make a comment that "she's not a lady"?

A. That's true. I made that statement.

Q. Can you explain what you meant by that statement?

A. Well, I've worked with Ms. Joyce in the past in the West Yard, and I have never heard a lady use the type of language that Ms. Joyce uses. And her actions at times, my personal feelings were that she did not act as a lady, as I know a lady to be.

Q. When you say type of language, you're talking about rough language?

A. I'm talking about, yes, I'm talking about a lot of very vulgar-type profanity.

Q. Would you say that that is the language that's used on the roads with some frequency?

A. It is amongst men, yes.

Q. Did you feel that your perception of her as not a lady influenced you in any manner in the making of your recommendation?

A. No, sir. It did not.

Woodside excused Baldanzi, and Dawson wisely decided to forego any further questioning and instead moved on to his remaining witnesses.

First came Clyde Davis, a road superintendent for the county, who had been a member of the second panel. Dawson led him through a fairly detailed account of how the panel had operated, what questions had been asked, whether notes had been made, and the fact that the panelists had not discussed the interviews until after the last applicant had been seen.

Q. Do you remember discussing Diane Joyce after the interview with the other interviewers?

A. No more than we did any other applicant, no.

Q. Do you remember making mention of her gender after the interview?

A. No. Her gender was apparent.

Q. Do you remember making mention of her union activities after the interview?

A. No. That was apparent also. It's a well-known fact.

Davis had, earlier in his career, held a dispatcher position, although it had not been called that at the time, so he could speak of its requirements with some familiarity, and he, too, described it as primarily clerical in function. Moreover, he had served on several other review panels, so he could assure the court that this one had been carried out in exactly the same way as the others. And when the panel had compared notes at the end, "The consensus was Mr. Johnson was number one unanimously. . . . A clear-cut favorite."

Davis had been a strong witness for Johnson, cool, calm, professional, and he bolstered Dawson's strategy of showing Paul Johnson as the best-qualified candidate of the seven. Woodside tried to shake that image by linking Davis to Baldanzi as part of the old-boy crowd.

Q. You indicated, in response to questions as to her gender, that her gender was apparent. Can you explain that?

A. Yes, she's a female.

Q. Was that in any way unusual, or did that strike you as being a factor in your decision-making?

A. Not in the least.

Q. Not in the least. What about her union activity?

A. That affected me not in the least.

Q. Mr. Baldanzi testified just a moment ago that he perceived Ms. Joyce as using rough or vulgar language. Do you have the same perception?

A. I do not.

Q. You do not? Can you characterize the type of language that she uses from day to day in the course of her work?

A. In my opinion, she uses normal language from day to day.

Woodside spent a few more minutes trying to show up some discrepancies in Davis's testimony and then gave up.

Dawson next called Humbert Anthony Di Basilio, whom Diane Joyce had painted in her testimony as the man who had set the process up in Paul Johnson's favor and who had been infuriated when she had received the post. Dawson questioned Di Basilio closely on his role in filling a vacancy and determined that he had had nothing to do with it until the creation of the second interview panel. As for its makeup, he had had only five men from which to choose three, so there had been very little discretion. As to charges that he had not been helpful to Diane Joyce in either informing her of the interview time or scheduling it to help her meet her other obligations, Di Basilio said he could not remember. Nor could he remember whether he had ever discussed Paul Johnson with the members of the second panel. But he did know that in the twenty-six years he had been with the roads the recommendations of review panels, especially strong recommendations such as in this case, had rarely been overridden. And he also knew that Mr. Graebner never bothered with appointments at this level of the organization and that the affirmative action office had never interfered in any other promotion.

Di Basilio had said several times that he had considered Paul Johnson the most qualified of the candidates, and he had heartily endorsed the panel's selection. Woodside spent some time sparring with Di Basilio to try to show bias and that Johnson's selection had been preplanned, but to no avail.

After lunch, Dawson called his last two witnesses, Myra Beals, who had been a personnel officer in the Transportation Agency in 1980 and responsible for implementation of the affirmative action plan. She proved a reluctant witness, and Dawson had to remind her constantly of what she had said in her earlier deposition about the county wanting women and other underrepresented groups to have greater opportunities, especially in the road system. She conceded that she had helped to put together written comments on Johnson and Joyce for the memorandum that would be used to confirm Joyce's hiring.

An essential part of any rationalization for an affirmative action program is that it addresses and remedies past discriminatory practices. Woodside had been intimating throughout his questioning that women had been discriminated against in the roads division. If Dawson could show that there had been little impediment to hiring women, whatever the numerical discrepancies might be, he could bolster his case considerably. He asked Myra Beals if, during her more than seven years working for the Transportation Agency, she had been aware of any practices specifically discriminatory against women.

She remembered a few cases that came to her on complaints and the fact that statistics pointed to continued underrepresentation of women and other minorities in certain EEOC categories, but she could not point to evidence of particular discriminatory practices.

Q. Do you remember the percentage of women in the Transportation Agency as a whole increasing during that period of time [when you were affirmative action coordinator]?

A. I can't say. I don't remember.

Q. So you can't say if the percentage of women increased in the Transportation Agency as a whole between 1980 and the present, either?

A. No, I can't.

Q. Did you ever look into why there were so few women in the road maintenance division?

A. As a specific topic, no, I can't recall doing that.

Dawson then turned to the question of goals in the county plan, and over the next several minutes elicited some of the most damaging testimony of the entire trial against the county plan. In fall 1978, the total county work force had been 22.4 percent women, and in its affirmative action plan, Santa Clara County had set an overall goal of 36.4 percent. That goal had been standard across every EEOC category, regardless of the current percentage of women already in that area, and without reference to the number of women in the available work force in the area who could qualify for those jobs.* The plan, moreover, had no end date and could go on indefinitely.

In certain areas, such as clerical and office help, which were predominantly staffed by women, the plan would not apply because the goals had been met. But if a white male applied for any of those positions, even if white males were underrepresented in that category, there would be no application of the plan because white males did not fall into any of the protected groups. Further, when pressed about whether there had been meetings to train county officials in implementing the plan, Beals could remember only one such meeting. All

* This issue, which played a relatively minor role in the trial, would be a major topic in oral argument at the Supreme Court. If an employer sets goals at a percentage of women or minorities in the overall work force, one assumes that the jobs will be for the most part unskilled. If the jobs are skilled, than the realistic plan is to determine what percentage of minorities have the necessary skills. The county had classified the dispatcher as a skilled position, but its affirmative action plan seemed to rely on the total number of women in the local work force. This disjuncture bothered several of the justices; see chapter 8.

{ *Affirmative Action on Trial* }

in all, Dawson succeeded in eliciting from an ardent defender of affirmative action rather damning admissions that the plan had rigid goals and no terminal date and that there seemed to have been little if any training provided for its implementation.

Woodside could do little to repair that damage, so he stuck to his strategy of portraying the Transportation Agency as rife with discrimination, against women in general and against Diane Joyce in particular. Myra Beals recalled handling a complaint from Joyce in which a co-worker had harassed her and threatened to run her off with a forklift; and when Beals had met with three of the male managers, they had conceded that they knew about the situation and had done nothing about it. As one of them had said, "If it had been two men, they would have gone outside and fought it out and settled it." Beals told a few more stories to illustrate the antifemale bias of the road workers, but the incidents taken together could not establish the basic prerequisite of remedial affirmative action plans — the existence of a persistent discriminatory policy.

Dawson attempted to drive the last nails into the coffin with his final witness, Jan Davis, the woman currently responsible for affirmative action in the Transportation Agency. She confirmed that under the most recent revision of the plan, the county still called for 36.4 percent women in each category, a goal she believed unreasonable in some areas. When asked what categories she had in mind, Davis mentioned skilled crafts, because there were not enough women in the work force trained for that type of work. The agency's personnel office had been conducting extensive recruitment for road maintenance workers, but so far few women had expressed interest.

Dawson then asked her the same question he had asked Myra Beals: was she aware of any practice that she would consider discriminatory against women? No, she responded, no practice, although there had been isolated events.

When he tried to lead the witness through a review of how many incidents of promotion or appointment had been made because of affirmative action, Judge Ingram cut him off and wanted to know what value such evidence had. Dawson started to explain that he wanted to show how unusual the Joyce appointment had been, but then stopped; he had hammered that theme throughout the trial, and there was no sense in irritating the judge over a point already made.

He ended his questioning, and when Woodside indicated that he had no questions for the witness, Ingram called a short recess.

———

In his closing argument, Dawson claimed that the evidence showed two things. First, "but for the fact that there was a woman on the list, Mr. Johnson would have been appointed to the position." Ingram interrupted to say that was certainly clear, since Mr. Graebner had testified to that effect. That being the case, Dawson continued, then sex had been the determining factor, and under Title VII, "there has to be a very, very good reason to make employment decisions based upon sex, as it would be on race, or any other characteristic." He repeated that Johnson did not intend to challenge affirmative action, only the Transportation Agency plan and its application in his case, and Dawson ticked off the problems that had been revealed about the plan. "There has to be some reasonable basis to use sex or race in any type of employment decision. We submit there isn't in this case."

Dawson claimed that it had been shown conclusively that Paul Johnson had been the best qualified applicant for the job, and to deny him what he deserved under the county's own merit criteria required that the county put forward some compelling reason.

> Dawson: We say No, you can't use sex, you can't use discretion, if you're the appointing authority, if you're anyone who falls under Title VII laws, unless you can tie that act into underrepresentation caused by an act of this entity, or something that is very serious and egregious, something that's well-known, like in *Weber*, the fact that blacks in the South do not get into skilled-craft positions. We simply don't think that's the case here.
>
> Judge Ingram: In other words, it's your point that in order to have a good enough reason to violate Title VII, they have to remedy some wrong that they were active in perpetrating, is that right, or some widespread social problem, such as black people in the South?
>
> Dawson: There has to be some nexus, Your Honor, between the entity itself and the underrepresentation. It can't just be general societal discrimination.

Judge Ingram: Well, in other words, if nobody applies to work on the roads that's a woman because — for any reason, other than one induced by the county, then that would not be a good enough reason, if that's what resulted in the underrepresentation.

Dawson: That's correct, Your Honor.

Whether Stephen Woodside recognized it or not at this point, the momentum in the trial had swung over to Paul Johnson. James Dawson had done his work well; he had managed to keep the focus of the trial on his client. He had portrayed Paul Johnson as the most qualified person for the job, ranked that way through the county's own personnel procedures, and a less qualified person had been appointed for one reason and one reason only — gender. This blatant discrimination violated federal law, and his client deserved to be made whole for the wrong done to him.

Woodside had been dancing along a very thin line throughout the trial, and he recognized that he would have to be more explicit if he had any hope of winning his case in summation. The affirmative action plan could be justified for only one reason, if the county had in fact purposely discriminated against women. He started going over the incidents of discrimination that had been mentioned as well as the statistics showing underrepresentation when Judge Ingram interrupted him and asked point blank, "Was the county responsible in some fashion, through discriminatory policy, for an underrepresentation of women?"

Woodside could not do the one thing that might have given him a chance, make an admission of overt discrimination, so he intimated that the county had allowed discrimination to take place and pointed to some exhibits showing the extent of underrepresentation.

Woodside: I think, as Your Honor is aware, statistics play a very prominent role in Title VII litigation. Certainly in class action litigation, it's oftentimes the most decisive factor.

Judge Ingram: A less decisive role in individual litigation.

Woodside: Yes, but nonetheless, a relevant role. I believe you can say that if there's a statistical aberration, that may tend to prove discrimination in an individual case.

Judge Ingram: I think you can use it to corroborate other evidentiary acts of discrimination, but I don't — it can't carry the day, as it can in the class action, by itself.

Woodside: That's correct, Your Honor. That's correct.

Trying to recover the momentum, Woodside went back to the argument he had been trying to make throughout the trial, that Paul Johnson was not that much better qualified than Diane Joyce, and that since both had qualified for finalists, the hiring authority could take into account other criteria, including gender as it related to the affirmative action plan. Plaintiff's evidence, Woodside contended, just did not prove that Johnson had a right to that job. Before he could go on, Judge Ingram interrupted again to press him on the county's plan.

> Judge Ingram: The evidence does not reveal any termination of this affirmative action plan. And there's no question but what the affirmative action plan sanctions racial and sexual discrimination, and thus violates Title VII. Right?
>
> Woodside: It sanctions, Your Honor, that consideration be given to gender where there's underrepresentation.
>
> Judge Ingram: Which is contrary to federal law.
>
> Woodside: You're right, it's discrimination based on sex.
>
> Judge Ingram: This is going to be going on in perpetuity.
>
> Woodside: First of all, Your Honor, it is not. Our plan, unlike some others, sets up no quota system. There's no requirement that one out of three —
>
> Judge Ingram: It sets percentage goals, apparently.
>
> Woodside: Okay, they are goals. . . . And the plan, if you look at it from a perspective of 1978, is that that's our goal, and we're going to set out to try to do that with no particular termination date.
>
> Judge Ingram: Is there anything in evidence before me from which I can tell how long the thing is going to last?
>
> Woodside: Nothing at this point, Your Honor, that's in evidence.

Judge Ingram kept pushing Woodside about the imprecision of the plan in so many areas, about how it would impact upon individual males in the future, about when and how would the county know if it had been successful. The county's counsel struggled valiantly, but even if he had wanted to answer more precisely, the fact became evident that there were no answers to some of these questions. Ingram, in just a few short moments, had put his finger on every weakness of the Santa Clara County affirmative action plan.

James Dawson and Steven Woodside had one more task to perform for Judge Ingram; each had to prepare a proposed "findings and conclusion" memorandum, setting out what each client wanted should the judge decide in his or her favor. The county merely wanted Paul Johnson's suit dismissed and its personnel decision affirmed, leaving both Diane Joyce in her job and the affirmative action plan in place. Paul Johnson asked for the county to promote him to dispatcher and to pay him the difference in wages between what he had earned in his current job and what he would have earned as dispatcher in the two years since the event, as well as reasonable attorney fees for James Dawson. The memoranda also had to support these findings in terms of the facts presented at the trial and the relevant law.

Both men turned in their proposals to the court within a week after the trial ended in May and then waited almost three months while Judge Ingram wrestled with the problem. The facts made it clear enough that Paul Johnson had been discriminated against on the basis of his sex, a violation of Title VII of the Civil Rights Act. The testimony also seemed to support his contention that he had been the better qualified of the two, although the county did have the right to choose any of the qualified finalists. Yet the Supreme Court in *Weber* had approved race- or gender-conscious plans that responded to a record of past discrimination, and in an earlier line of cases had endorsed the use of statistical imbalances as proof of discrimination.

Ingram was not about to start second-guessing the county's personnel department on whether the dispatcher should be rated as skilled or clerical; that classification had been made well before Diane Joyce had applied for the job. In any event, courts should not be involved in such questions, so long as the agency's personnel policies followed accepted practice and had been applied fairly and in a consistent manner. So if he accepted the county's rating of the job as skilled, then he would also have to accept the county's statistics showing no women in a skilled-job category that employed 238 men. From this perspective, as the county had argued, one could infer discrimination and justify the affirmative action plan.

But Ingram had trouble, not with the concept of affirmative action, but with the county plan. The goal of 36.4 percent women in every job category had been admitted by one of the county's own personnel officers as unrealistic. Moreover, it appeared so rigid as to be less a "goal" and more of a "quota," which, except in rare cases of blatant discrimination, the Supreme Court had refused to endorse. The open-ended nature of the plan also bothered him, along with the wide discretion given to individual hiring officers to fine-tune the program as it went along.

In early August the clerk of the court called Woodside and Dawson to tell them that Judge Ingram had reached his decision and wanted to meet with them. When they arrived in his chambers, he laid it out very simply. The county's affirmative action plan did not measure up to the *Weber* criteria; Paul Johnson, therefore, should be promoted and should receive the differential in pay ($5,654.48), and the amount of attorney's fees would be computed later. Ingram's ruling relied almost entirely on Dawson's proposed findings, but the judge did not accept his rationales. He finessed the questions of job classification and statistical imbalance by relying on the plan's defects, a strategy that allowed him to reach this decision but that would become an issue later.

"I'll never forget Steve's face," Dawson later recalled. "I mean, it was the biggest shock in the world that he had lost the case, since it's sort of difficult to lose in a Title VII defense case if you represent a public institution."

The decision awarded Paul Johnson what he had asked for and vindicated his claim that he had earned the job and then had been deprived of it because of discrimination. Although the county would drag its feet in implementing the decree, it could also breathe a sign of relief that Ingram had handed down a fairly narrow ruling. The county affirmative action plan remained intact, and future suits of this kind could easily be avoided by some simple and straightforward changes in the plan and its rationale. The county could live with that.

A jubilant Jim Dawson left Ingram's chambers to give his client the good news. Steve Woodside reported back to 70 Henning Street, the county government's headquarters, to tell his boss and the county executive that they had lost and what they now had to do. When Diane Joyce learned about the decision, she called the union.

CHAPTER 5

The Road to the Marble Palace

When Kristy Sermersheim picked up her phone, she heard an agitated Diane Joyce exclaim, "We lost!" "What do you mean, we lost?" Kristy asked. "Ann Ravel said it wasn't even going to go to trial. Do you mean it went to trial?" Joyce told the SEIU representative what she knew and then waited to learn not only whether the union would help her, but what the county planned to do in response to Judge Ingram's order.

After hanging up, Sermersheim ran down the hall, burst into Michael Baratz's office, and demanded that the union do something. "They're going to kick Diane out," she said, "and we can't let this happen. She's entitled to the appointment under the rule of seven, and the boss was nuts not to pick her in the first place. It's because she's smart, and she's a woman, and she's a steward. The union has to help her." Aside from questions of principle, Sermersheim said, the whole case smacked of union bashing, "of a union steward getting ousted by a heavy-duty, really anti-union non-member man."

Baratz agreed something had to be done, but so far the union had not been involved in the case. While Local 715 of the State Employees' International Union backed affirmative action, it would be better if the county showed a real commitment to the concept by defending its own plan. Baratz began to make some phone calls, and as he later recalled, discovered that the Board of Supervisors had little interest in appealing. Both Suzanne Wilson and Rod Diardon, whom the union considered liberal and friendly to labor interests, reported that the county counsel had advised the board that an appeal could open a can of worms that could scuttle the entire affirmative action plan.

Steven Woodside remembers the story somewhat differently and claims that from the beginning the board stood willing to appeal

Ingram's decision. Even before the briefing by the counsel, one member, Rebecca Morgan, had come to the conclusion that the judge had been wrong and that the county should fight the ruling. The judge had not even looked at the statistics, which in her opinion showed a definite bias against women, and she strongly disagreed with Ingram that the lack of a specific end date made the plan defective. And that, according to Woodside, "was the reaction of the whole board."

Eventually the Board of Supervisors did decide to fight, but the evidence seems to support the union view that it took some pressure to achieve that result. Several weeks passed and nothing happened; the union suspected that Woodside was dragging his feet and decided to force his hand by making a public appeal to the supervisors. The board, at its regular Tuesday morning meeting, had a so-called "one-minute calendar," an opportunity for people not on the regular agenda to request consideration of a particular issue. Michael Baratz told Kristy Sermersheim to get on the one-minute calendar.

She went to the meeting the next Tuesday, and when her turn came, asked the board if they knew that the county had only two more weeks to appeal Judge Ingram's decision. Diane Joyce, she reminded them, had been picked in pursuance of the affirmative action plan, and now she would be out. Were they going to do anything about this? This news, she recalled, seemed a big surprise to the board, and several members looked quite startled by it. They promised to "get back" with her, the standard reply to one-minute requests, but a day or so later, Suzanne Wilson came over to the union's headquarters, a few blocks from the county seat. After discussing the case for a while, she said, "This is really a problem, isn't it?" Yes, it is, they agreed.

Wilson went back to the board, which now agreed that the county counsel should file an appeal. Local 715, in the meantime, decided that it needed to get more involved. Since it had not been a party to the original suit, it had no standing to present arguments or file appeals. If the county had decided not to pursue the case, the union would have been unable to do anything about it. Michael Baratz first went to speak with David Rosenfeld, a San Francisco labor attorney whose firm had long represented the SEIU, to find out what options the union had. He learned that in order to have a voice before the courts, the union had to intervene in the suit and in essence become a party to the case. "If we intervene," Rosenfeld told him, "then the county can't screw it up any more, since we can be there watching what is happening."

Baratz then went to the governing board of Local 715 to explain what had happened and to emphasize the importance of backing Diane Joyce for the sake of affirmative action. He also told them that he doubted the will, and by implication the competence, of the county counsel and asked the board to authorize Dave Rosenfeld to intervene on its behalf. Just as Jim Dawson represented Paul Johnson, so Dave Rosenfeld would now be working to protect Diane Joyce. After a brief discussion, the board agreed that Rosenfeld should proceed and that it would pay the necessary legal expenses. Even while county officials had been debating whether to act, Rosenfeld had filed a motion with Judge Ingram to allow Local 715 to intervene; after a brief hearing on October 25, 1982, Ingram ordered that the union could intervene solely for the purposes of arguing a motion for a new trial and participating in any appeals taken by the county to a higher court, but for no other purpose.

Judge Ingram had handed down his decree on August 10, 1982, and denied a rehearing on October 27; at that time he gave the county until December 27 to file an appeal in the Ninth Circuit. As Christmas approached, Steven Woodside hurried to write his brief. Dave Rosenfeld prepared the SEIU brief, setting forth the union's interest in the case and why it believed the district court decision to have been wrong. Michael Baratz kept up the political pressure on the Board of Supervisors to maintain its interest in affirmative action and dispatched his assistant, Kristy Sermersheim, to keep Diane Joyce calm and focused. In the meantime, an increasingly angry Jim Dawson wanted to know why the county was dragging its feet in implementing Ingram's decree giving Paul Johnson the dispatcher's mike.

———

In preparing his brief for the appeal, Woodside faced the same problem that had bedeviled him at the trial, how to defend a program based on an assumption of prior bias without admitting that the county had, in fact, discriminated against women. He could not, and did not — with one exception — challenge the findings of fact, since there had been no disagreement at the trial over what had happened, only about how the facts should be interpreted. The county did challenge Judge Ingram's finding the affirmative action plan defective because of its allegedly open-ended nature, but by itself this did not appear to be sufficient grounds on which to reverse the ruling. James Dawson described the county's appellate brief as "a perfunctory effort at best . . . not a very good brief." In his reply, he pointed out that appeals had to be based either on law or on fact and that a disagreement with a judge's interpretation of one aspect of the record did not constitute sufficient grounds for reversal. The case had been docketed by the clerk of the court of appeals on January 19, 1983, and all the briefs and replies had been filed by the end of July. Now the attorneys waited until the court could schedule a hearing.

Looking back a year after the case had been decided in the Supreme Court, Dawson admits that he went up to the Ninth Circuit "overly confident," sure that he could not lose. Events prior to the actual hearing bolstered this sense of victory. In the Ninth Circuit, staff attorneys who work for the court meet with both sides to see if a settlement can be reached so that the time and expense of a full panel can be avoided. When the staff attorney met with Dawson, Woodside, and Rosenfeld in fall 1983, he asked Woodside why he was even bothering to appeal. Rosenfeld, however, jumped in and said there could be no settlement, because the union wanted to uphold the affirmative action plan.

A short time later, both sides received notice that their case, Docket No. 83-1532, would be heard on February 14, 1984, at 9:00 A.M. The case also had an asterisk next to it, indicating that the court had placed it on the so-called short calendar, in which both sides together had only fifteen minutes to present their arguments. Attorneys practicing in the Ninth Circuit knew that a case on the short calendar meant the judges did not see any major mistakes in the lower court decision, and there would be little chance of reversing the original ruling. Dawson figured that he would be finished at 9:15, 9:30 at the latest, and planned to take the rest of the day off, visiting some friends in San Francisco and perhaps doing a little shopping. Steve Woodside and David Rosenfeld also knew what the asterisk meant—Woodside termed it the "kiss of death"—and realized that unless something dramatic happened in oral argument, they had little chance of winning on their appeal.

When a case is appealed from a federal district court to a circuit court, it is heard by a panel of three judges drawn from the larger number of judges appointed to that court. Case 83-1532 had been assigned to a panel consisting of J. Clifford Wallace, Warren J. Ferguson, and Betty M. Fletcher.

Wallace, the senior of the three, had been appointed to the court of appeals in 1972. A native of San Diego, he had practiced law there from 1955 to 1970, when President Nixon named him to the federal district court; two years later, Nixon elevated him to the Ninth Circuit. One of the most conservative members of that court, he wrote in his *Who's Who* entry that "my principles, ideals and goals, and my standard of conduct are embodied in the Gospel of Jesus Christ. They come to fruition in family life, service, industry and integrity, and in an attempt in some small way to make my community a better place within which to live." In 1988, following the Senate rejection of Robert Bork to the high court, the Reagan administration considered Wallace as a possible appointee, but in the end chose his colleague, Anthony Kennedy. David Rosenfeld described Wallace as a judge with a conservative agenda but very bright and courteous to all the attorneys who argued before him.

At the other end of the ideological spectrum stood Judge Betty M. Fletcher of Seattle. An extremely bright woman, she had graduated with honors from Stanford but did not enter law school for another decade. She then practiced law in her hometown until President Carter named her to the court in 1979. A friend and admirer of William O. Douglas, she shared many of his interests and political views as well.

In the middle stood Warren J. Ferguson, another 1979 Carter appointee. A native of Nevada, he had moved to California after service in World War II and built up a successful practice in Fullerton, a growing community south of Los Angeles. In 1959 he held the first of several state court positions, and President Johnson named him to the federal district court in 1966. During his years of private practice as well as after he became a judge, Ferguson taught law as an adjunct instructor at several area law schools. A man with a wry sense of humor, he declared that he had adopted as his philosophy of life the old Nevada miner's creed: "Live today; look every man in the eye; and tell the rest of the world to go to hell."

An observer could reasonably anticipate that Wallace would not be overly sympathetic to affirmative action, Fletcher would be, and the decision, then, would rest with the centrist Ferguson. Like any good appellate judge, however, he would have to be convinced that sufficient grounds existed to overturn the lower court decision. Dawson did not know any of the three, but Rosenfeld, who had argued often in the Ninth Circuit, believed that Ferguson could be won over, and he and Woodside, for the first time, saw a glimmer of hope. It would depend, however, on whether Woodside could catch the court's attention and move at least two of the judges to believe that the lower court had decided the case incorrectly.

Woodside began his argument by noting that employers in cases like this one faced litigation one way or the other. If one went by the disparity in numbers, then women and minorities could sue on the grounds that they had been systematically excluded. If in an effort to open up opportunities the employer established an affirmative action program, it faced claims of reverse discrimination by white males. Before he could get very far with this argument, Judge Wallace interrupted him with a question about the facts. Rather than fazing him, the question bolstered Woodside's confidence; he had studied the record until he knew it cold and could practically cite the pages on which the court would find this particular set of numbers.

As Wallace pushed on, Ferguson and Fletcher began listening more closely, and soon they joined in as well. The fifteen minutes allotted to the case passed, and the questioning went on, first Woodside, then Rosenfeld, then Dawson. Wallace pressed Woodside: if the county made employment decisions on the basis of race, sex, or some other characteristic, then did it not have a very heavy burden to bear in the nature of an affirmative defense, that is, proof of prior discrimination as a justification for otherwise illegal practices? Did the facts support such a record? Woodside again had to avoid the pitfall of conceding prior discrimination lest he open the county to a flood of Title VII suits from women, blacks, and Hispanics. He could only point to the disparities shown by the numbers.

Betty Fletcher went after Jim Dawson as aggressively as Wallace had questioned Woodside. At one point in his argument he attacked the county plan as "social engineering," and she launched into what Dawson considered a tirade about "the march of history" and the "invisible impediments" that women and other minorities face. Dawson, whose practice includes a great deal of trial work, said he could not recall when he had ever been on the receiving end of so much hostility and ad hominem attacks from a results-oriented judge.

Judge Ferguson did his best to mediate between the two extremes and finally interrupted the proceedings to apologize to the other attorneys in the audience who had expected to march through their cases on the short calendar and get back to their offices. Evidently, Ferguson explained, we are not going to get through with this case for a while, and we will probably not hear any other cases until this afternoon.

At some point that morning, Paul Johnson's efforts to reverse what he considered the county's shameful treatment of him — what the lawyers involved termed a "minor" Title VII case — became something far bigger. As Jim Dawson later recalled, his whole effort had been on behalf of a client whom they both believed the county had wronged. The case "didn't seem important to me other than because of Paul Johnson, who for the first time in his life, was going against his employer. That was a tough thing for him to do. This was a case having to do with Paul Johnson; it had nothing to do with social policy."

Certainly the Ninth Circuit had not seen anything terribly significant in the case when it had assigned the appeal to the short calendar. The briefs filed by the county and the union had not questioned Ingram's decision on the basis of overarching policy questions; they believed he had erred in a relatively minor way. Jim Dawson had not raised large constitutional issues such as equal protection; he had won on Title VII grounds in the district court, and he saw no reason to change his tactics. The county also did not care to get into the equal protection morass, realizing it could backfire against it. All in all, the original judgment of the court in placing an asterisk next to Case No. 83-1532 appeared fully justified by the record.

By the time the oral argument ended, however, both sides realized that whether they had wanted to or not, they had stumbled into a legal and social minefield. Dawson still thought the panel would affirm Judge Ingram, but he appreciated that far larger issues surrounded Paul Johnson's suit than just remedying what one person perceived as a wrong done to him. Paul Johnson probably had understood from the start that if he could be stripped of a job that he believed he had won—had earned—on merit in order to placate a politically vocal minority, then not only would white males suffer, but the whole idea of merit and ability and perseverance as virtues to be rewarded would be lost. Johnson never considered himself an oppressor, part of a majority that had for decades discriminated against women and minorities because he personally had never seen himself involved in such bias. For him, this had begun as an individual complaint—he had been the victim of reverse discrimination—but he had intuitively understood the greater questions involved.

Diane Joyce, like Paul Johnson, recognized that the outcome of the case affected far more than her own job status. If affirmative action succeeded, women like her, who had been discriminated against throughout their lives for no reason other than gender, would now have a chance to be judged—just as Paul Johnson wanted to be—on merit alone. If affirmative action failed, then women and minorities would continue to be shut out of better-paying jobs and promotional opportunities, not because they lacked the ability but because they happened to be women or black or Hispanic. At least some of these issues had been raised in the oral argument; now Judges Ferguson, Fletcher, and Wallace would have to wrestle with them in deciding whether to affirm or reverse the lower court.

———

Normally, after a three-judge panel hears its morning cases, it will meet to take a preliminary vote and report the results to the senior judge on the circuit. The opinion will be assigned to one of the panel judges in the majority, and when ready, will be circulated to the other judges on the panel; if there is a disagreement over the result, the dissenting judge will also circulate his or her opinion. When the three are satisfied that the written opinions reflect their views accurately, the decision is released. In simple cases, the opinions may be very short and the results announced within a few weeks of the hearing; more complicated cases, or cases in which the judges have difficulty reaching or explaining their decision, may take many months. In *Johnson*, the panel heard the case on February 14, 1984, and did not hand down its decision until December 4, almost ten months later.

Judge Fletcher wrote the majority opinion, joined by Ferguson, reversing the lower court and upholding Santa Clara County's affirmative action plan as meeting the *Weber* guidelines. She ruled that Judge Ingram had interpreted Title VII and *Weber* too narrowly; Congress had specifically declared its hope that Title VII would trigger similar efforts at the local level, and the Supreme Court had indicated its willingness to permit some latitude in dealing with problems of prior discrimination.

All courts, state as well as federal, are bound by the decisions of the Supreme Court. But if the high court has not yet addressed a particular issue, the circuits may fashion their own remedies and look to their own precedents for guidance. In this case, the Ninth Circuit had an applicable precedent, *LaRiviere v. EEOC* (9th Cir. 1982), in which it had upheld an affirmative action plan to hire and train women as traffic officers to remedy a long-standing gender imbalance in the California Highway Patrol. The court had held that those individuals excluded from the plan because of their sex could not sue for redress since the plan operated consistently with the intent of Title VII. The Santa Clara plan, according to Judge Fletcher, had many characteristics similar to the Highway Patrol scheme the court had earlier approved.

As for Judge Ingram's concern that the county plan had no fixed end date, she noted that neither did it make any claims to permanency, and she believed the lower court had been misled by Graebner's description of the plan as "a permanent part of the agency's basic operating philosophy." She took that to mean only that in the future the agency would always be alert to gender or racial imbalances in the work force and would seek to avoid such problems. The plan, therefore, met the *Weber* criteria in that it had long-term goals, was remedial in nature, and did not unduly trammel the rights of white males. Although, unlike *Weber*, the Santa Clara plan did not create additional job opportunities, neither did it foreclose them. To view Diane Joyce's selection as a complete bar to future opportunities for Paul Johnson, she concluded, constituted far too narrow a view of what the county had tried to do and what the law permitted:

> We conclude that the Agency plan, like the *Weber* plan, "falls on the permissible side of the line." We hold that the Agency's selection of Joyce, pursuant to the plan, was a lawful effort to remedy an entrenched pattern of manifest imbalance. We are not unsym-

pathetic to the complaint of Johnson and others before our court that employers' attempts to remedy past discrimination sometimes visit burdens upon individual members of the non-minority group. As the Agency plan recognizes, however, "the mere existence of an opportunity for members of [discriminated] groups to apply for jobs . . . will *not* by itself result in timely attainment of parity for currently under-represented groups." Affirmative action is necessary and lawful, within the guidelines of *Weber*, to remedy longstanding imbalances in the work force.

As a result, the court reversed the lower court decision that had given Paul Johnson the dispatcher's mike; Graebner's selection of Diane Joyce would stand.

Judge Wallace concurred in part and dissented in part. He believed that the lower court had not explored the problem of numerical disparity sufficiently to warrant the court making "broad pronouncements of judicial policy," and he would have preferred remanding the case for further hearing. Wallace, however, disagreed with the majority's interpretation of Title VII. The "ultimate question," he noted, is "discrimination *vel non*. . . . The existence of an affirmative action plan does not change this essential inquiry."

When plaintiffs such as Johnson challenged promotion decisions under Title VII, they had to prove either disparate treatment — they had been treated unfairly because of specific criteria aimed against their group — or they had to show disparate impact — though the criteria did not explicitly single out their group, it had the same effect as if it had. Once the plaintiff has carried the burden of showing that he or she had been discriminated against, the employer could enter an affirmative defense that there had been past discrimination that had to be remedied by a legitimate affirmative action plan.

Wallace then went into a fairly rigorous analysis of what each side had to do, and what criteria courts should use to determine whether the plaintiff had met the minimal burden of proving discrimination, and what an employer had to show to justify an affirmative action plan as an affirmative defense. He faulted the majority for requiring only a vague showing of "some evidence" of a statistical disparity and "some evidence" that the plan addressed the imbalance. Wallace did not say that Ingram had been either right or wrong but merely that he had not asked the right questions and produced a sufficient record to justify either the lower court decision against the county or the appeals court reversal.

In terms of rigorous analysis, Wallace's opinion is unquestionably far more logical than Fletcher's. Technically, he did not disagree with the conclusion that the district court had erred:

> I cannot join this opinion, however, because I disagree with the majority's allocation of the burdens of persuasion and production, and because I believe that the district court should have the first opportunity to correct its own errors and conduct the intense factual analysis necessary to resolve these issues. In order for the majority to uphold the plan, it has taken several unnecessary doctrinal steps that weaken the Supreme Court's test in *Weber* as interpreted by *LaRiviere*. From these pronouncements, I dissent.

The purpose of his intense questioning of Steven Woodside had been to determine whether there had been past discrimination sufficient to justify an affirmative action plan, and that, of course, is what Woodside did not want to admit. Wallace did not oppose a bona fide plan, but numerical disparity, by itself, did not in his view justify a plan that did, in fact, discriminate against other groups. In many ways this position proved far more moderate than that of the Reagan administration, which would have allowed relief only to those actually discriminated against. Wallace would not, however, as the majority seemed willing to do, accept allegations of disparity as proof of discrimination.

———

The court of appeals had affirmed the Transportation Agency plan, but the county now had another problem. After dragging its feet for nearly a year, it had finally implemented Judge Ingram's decision and in late spring 1983 had given Paul Johnson the dispatcher's mike at the East Yard. To show its commitment to affirmative action, however, it had created another dispatcher's job by upgrading a position at the South Yard and had assigned Diane Joyce there. From her point of view this was a less than satisfactory arrangement, since it added on over forty miles of commuting every day; she wanted to return to her original assignment at the East Yard. The county, however, decided to leave Johnson and Joyce where they were and hoped the issue would die down. After all, Johnson had the dispatcher's job and the back pay he had sought and won in the district court, even though the court of appeals had overturned that ruling, and Joyce had the position and salary she had wanted. The county affirmative action plan seemed safe, and with the appellate decision another lawsuit appeared unlikely should a woman or minority be chosen over a white male in the future. Steven Woodside could take satisfaction that a good oral presentation had literally snatched victory out of the jaws of defeat. He assumed the Ninth Circuit decision would end the matter, and he prepared to close the file on the case and send the folder to storage.

Paul Johnson, however, felt frustrated. He had been vindicated by Judge Ingram, but the victory had been spoiled by the court of appeals. From his point of view, the appellate decision meant that under the law, one could discriminate against white males and they could do nothing about it. Even though he had the dispatcher's job, Johnson was too honest a man not to recognize that he was keeping the job only because the county hoped to keep things quiet.

Following the court of appeals decision, Dawson and Johnson had made one last effort, and on December 21, 1984, had asked the panel to rehear the case and suggested that the Ninth Circuit hear the case *en banc*. Under this procedure, the losing party in essence says that the decision of this particular three-judge panel does not correctly reflect either the law or the views of a majority of the members of the circuit, and had there been a different lineup, the result might have gone the other way. A case on appeal is supposed to be judged by the law, and theoretically the result should be the same no matter what the panel composition is. If a majority of the circuit judges disagrees with the panel decision, or if in a split decision it believes the law is unclear, it may agree to rehear the case with all the members of the circuit sitting together.

But just as a three-judge panel is unwilling to overturn a trial court decision unless there is clear error, so a full circuit is unwilling to rehear a case decided by three of its members unless there are significant problems with the result. Moreover, a rehearing *en banc* is not a right; a party may not "petition" but only "suggest" that it occur. It is then up to the dissenting judge whether that suggestion is circulated among his or her colleagues. If the dissenter feels strongly about the case and believes that a majority of his or her colleagues agrees, then the dissenter will attempt to secure the votes for an *en banc* hearing. Most circuit judges do not like to sit *en banc*, and it is a rare case when it happens.

Because of the importance of the questions, Fletcher and Ferguson agreed that the suggestion for an *en banc* hearing should be circulated, but none of their colleagues requested a vote. Although a majority of the circuit may or may not have agreed with the decision reached by Ferguson and Fletcher, the opinion appeared to conform to the general criteria of *Weber*, and the court refused to rehear the case. But in its denial of the petition for rehearing and the suggestion for an *en banc* on September 5, 1985, the panel in an unusual step amended its earlier opinions.

Fletcher added several short sections in an effort to show that her opinion did not take a casual attitude toward the requirements of a legitimate affirmative action plan and claimed that her analysis met the *Weber* criteria. Moreover, she claimed that Wallace had mistaken the law and incorrectly cited Justice Blackmun's concurrence in that case. This brought an angry retort from Wallace, and an addition to his opinion as well, that he had "correctly cited the law" and that the majority decision ran contrary to *Weber*.

A thoroughly disgusted Paul Johnson decided to call it quits, both on the case and on the job. At age sixty he had enough years of service and enough money saved to take early retirement, and while normally he would have worked until sixty-five, "I just wanted to get the hell out of there." He went to Dawson's office and told him to figure up his bill; it had been over five years since he had initiated the suit, and he could not afford to fight the case any more. Dawson understood the situation, but told Johnson that if he wanted to try to take the case to the Supreme Court, there were some public interest firms that might take it on. They would pay the costs and only needed his permission. "Fine," Johnson said, "but I can't afford any more."

Public interest law firms are a fairly new development in American law. Many lawyers devote some of their time to pro bono work, that is, work for a good cause for which they accept no remuneration. This may take the form of advising poor clients on civil law (family matters, bankruptcy, and so on) at a legal clinic or working with indigent prisoners on their appeals. Some attorneys, such as Louis D. Brandeis, devoted their time to representing reform groups or even cities and states in defense of particular programs. The efforts of the NAACP to break down the walls of segregation led to the creation of the NAACP Legal Defense Fund, Inc., a separate and independent entity that pursued only civil rights litigation and that depended for its financing almost entirely on donations. The "Inc. Fund" became the model for other public interest firms that specialized in such areas as women's rights, consumer protection, and the environment as well as some that had particular liberal or conservative ideological agendas.

Several conservative firms expressed an interest in Paul Johnson's case, and after looking over their credentials, Jim Dawson arranged a "beauty contest" between the Pacific Legal Foundation of Sacramento and the Denver-based Mountain States Legal Foundation, where both firms would meet with him and his client and they could decide who would get the case.

Looking back later, Dawson somewhat wistfully said he wished they had gone with Pacific, since it had appeared willing to allow him a larger role should the Supreme Court accept the case. But Mountain States seemed better qualified, and it boasted the talents of K. Preston Oade, who had recently argued a reverse discrimination case in the Supreme Court and who had a great deal of experience in affirmative action and employment discrimination law. Johnson and Dawson looked over his impressive resumé, as well as copies of decisions in cases he had won. If Mountain States took the case, it would pick up all the costs, but it would also have sole control of the appeal. Their attorneys would consult with Jim Dawson, but they would have the final word on the structure of the appeal and would handle oral argument. Dawson did not particularly care for this arrangement, but both he and Johnson thought Oade the best qualified person to argue the case. Dawson agreed to take the backseat, and Johnson signed a consent form to allow Mountain States to appeal the circuit court decision to the U.S. Supreme Court. Shortly afterward, Preston Oade left Mountain States.

Thereafter, Paul Johnson's case would be handled by Constance Brooks, who had joined Mountain States as a senior attorney in 1982. After graduating from Tulane Law School in 1977, she had worked for a private law firm in Washington, D.C., and had been fascinated by the public interest litigation that it did as part of its larger work. But as she grew more experienced, it became, as she put it, less cost-effective for the firm to assign her to that type of case. Mountain States offered her not only a chance to return to her native Colorado but also the full-time opportunity to do public interest work. Brooks found the atmosphere at Mountain States congenial in a number of ways. While it supported conservative economic ideas, it also endorsed libertarian positions on many social issues and thus could, and at times did, find itself allied in certain causes with the American Civil Liberties Union.

Attorneys at the firm read about Paul Johnson's case, and then the four senior attorneys discussed whether it constituted the type of litigation the firm should join. At one time Mountain States did "cradle-to-grave" work, initiating a suit for a plaintiff and carrying it through to the last appeal. But with limited resources and rapidly changing case law, the firm had adopted a strategy of involvement at particular stages, where it believed its assistance could be most effective. By 1982, Mountain States had been involved in several types of reverse discrimination suits, and its attorneys wanted to help Paul Johnson if he agreed.

In addition to her role as head of the section on natural resource litigation, Brooks at the time served as supervising attorney at Mountain States, directing the relatively young staff in various procedures, so she had the initial responsibility for overseeing preparation of petitions for certiorari. When Oade left, only two attorneys, she and Diane Vaksdal, knew anything about Johnson's case, so they stepped in full-time to finish the cert petition. Since most of the staff had been out of law school only a few years, Brooks was also one of the few lawyers at Mountain States with the five years of practice required for admission to the Supreme Court bar. She had not yet met Paul Johnson or James Dawson; over the next eighteen months she would get to know them well.

———

Under the rules of the Supreme Court, the losing party in a lower court has ninety days from the time of final judgment in which to file a petition for a writ of certiorari, thus initiating the process by which the Supreme Court will decide whether it will accept a case on appeal. Despite the famous litigant's cry of "I'll fight this all the way to the Supreme Court," very few cases are actually heard in the Court's marble palace across from the Capitol.

Cases come to the Supreme Court in one of three ways. The Constitution confers so-called "original jurisdiction" in a handful of instances, and in these cases, such as suits between two or more states or those "affecting Ambassadors, other public Ministers and Consuls," the suit is filed directly with the Court, which will act as a trial court. In all other cases, the Supreme Court has "appellate jurisdiction," and parties appeal from the highest tribunal either in a state or a federal court. There are two types of appellate jurisdiction. In a rare number of instances, a losing party has an automatic right to have the high court review the decision. This does not mean that the Court will actually hear oral arguments in these cases; nearly all the time it will rely on the briefs and dispose of the case summarily, issuing a terse statement usually upholding the decision below.

The vast majority of appeals to the Court come as petitions for certiorari, which the Court has discretion to accept or reject. The justices receive over 5,000 petitions for cert each term; of these they accept only a few hundred, many of which are disposed of summarily, either through upholding the lower court and thus affirming a particular point of law; overturning the lower court decision, a common procedure in the 1960s and 1970s in civil rights cases but otherwise fairly rare; or remanding (sending the case back to a lower court) for further review in light of a particular and usually recent Supreme Court decision. Perhaps 150 cases a year will receive a full-dress consideration, including oral argument before the bench.

By the time Dawson and Johnson had chosen Mountain States, and Connie Brooks had been assigned the case, very little time remained of the ninety-day limit on filing an appeal, and Brooks realized that even working round-the-clock with assistance, she would not be able to file an effective appeal before December 4, 1985. So she requested a thirty-day extension from Associate Justice William H. Rehnquist, in his capacity as circuit justice for the Ninth Circuit. Rehnquist granted the extension, and Brooks filed the petition for writ of certiorari in the case of Paul E. Johnson, Petitioner, versus Transportation Agency, Santa Clara County, California, and Service

Employees International Union, Local 715, Respondents, on December 31, 1985, three days before the extended deadline. At the top of the title page, the clerk of the Court penciled in the docket number, 85-1129, the petition being number 1129 of those filed in the 1985 term of the Court. The petition listed Constance H. Brooks and Diane L. Vaksdal of Mountain States and James L. Dawson as the attorneys for Johnson, with Brooks as counsel of record.

Johnson, through his attorneys, asked the Court to grant the petition on two grounds. First, a conflict existed between two circuits. The Ninth Circuit decision in *Johnson* apparently held that a public employer could make gender-based employment decisions under cover of an affirmative action plan adopted solely on the basis of a statistical imbalance between men and women in the work force and without any evidence of overt discrimination. The Seventh Circuit, in a decision dealing with minority hiring in the South Bend, Indiana, police and fire departments, had ruled that statistical disparity by itself did not justify an affirmative action plan; there had to be proof of actual past discrimination (*Janowiak v. South Bend*, 7th Cir. 1984). Brooks had firm ground on this point, because it is one of the functions of the Supreme Court to resolve differences of interpretation among the circuits so that all citizens, no matter where they live, will be subject to the same federal law.

In her second justification, she challenged the Ninth Circuit panel's conclusion that the Santa Clara plan did not violate the criteria for voluntary affirmative action plans set out in *Weber*, which since its announcement in 1979 had been the standard by which lower courts evaluated affirmative action plans. Brooks read *Weber* to hold that there had to be past discrimination "so egregious that the Court could take judicial notice," and the plan had to be designed to break down the "old patterns" of segregation and hierarchy. Beyond that, the plan could not "unnecessarily trammel the interests of white employees" and would end when the current exclusion of minorities had been remedied. None of these conditions, she claimed, existed in this case:

> First, the district court found as a matter of fact and law that no discrimination against women had occurred, based on evidence and testimony presented by the Agency. Instead, the plan is based solely on statistical disparity. The plan is not intended to break

down traditional patterns of exclusion, because exclusionary acts have never occurred. The plan has neither an end date nor criteria to determine the end date. In more than seven years, the percentage goals in the plan have never been reviewed, nor has any yearly review been completed as the plan requires. Thus, the plan unnecessarily trammels the interests of the male employees because it has no remedial purpose.

Brooks had made no reference to equal protection, because the trial had been conducted strictly on Title VII grounds. If her only argument had been that the county plan did not square with the *Weber* holding, the chances of the Court accepting the case would have been slim. The Ninth Circuit had interpreted the facts and what *Weber* required in a way that did not seem blatantly mistaken; a majority of the judges had apparently thought the panel sufficiently right to preclude an *en banc* hearing. The need to resolve a difference between two circuits, however, would always receive close scrutiny by the bench. Whether in order to resolve that difference required a full-scale argument or merely a summary decision constituted another question.

Steven Woodside had not expected an appeal, and the first he knew that Mountain States had taken over Paul Johnson's case came when he learned that Connie Brooks had requested an extension of time. He was not too concerned, since he knew that the Court accepted only a small number of cases for review. But he did have to be admitted to the Supreme Court bar, a simple procedure he arranged by mail, so he could file a response to the petition.

Santa Clara County had had only one other case go up to the Supreme Court, but that had been a question of criminal procedure under California state law, and the appeal had been handled by the state attorney general. The county counsel's office had had absolutely no experience at all with the U.S. Supreme Court, but after a brief discussion, the county counsel, Donald Clark, decided Steven Woodside should keep control of the case. He had argued it at trial and successfully turned around the appellate court; most important, no one knew the record better than he did.

Woodside displayed a fair degree of self-confidence throughout the case, but he also had a good sense of his own strengths and limitations. He had trial experience and had argued a few cases before the Ninth Circuit, so he knew what had to be done at those levels. He recognized that at the Supreme Court inexperience would be a serious liability, and from the initial response to the petition for cert continuing through preparation for oral argument, he sought and accepted advice from others. He prepared a response to Johnson's petition and circulated it among his colleagues in the county counsel's office as well as to several outside lawyers for their reaction. They thought he had done a good job in hitting the right points.

Just as Connie Brooks had framed the key question to favor her argument, so Woodside now did the same. "May an employer," he asked,

> consider gender as a factor in promoting a qualified woman where none of 238 persons employed in the job category were female and where the employer's voluntary affirmative action plan set no quotas, but permitted gender to be a factor in employment decisions until such time as the employer's work force is representative of the local area labor force?

Woodside's two key points responded directly to those raised by Brooks. The court of appeals decision, he maintained, had been consistent with the standards enunciated in *Weber* and presented no facts that would give rise to a new issue requiring review by the Court. He narrated the events emphasizing how the county plan had responded to a particular set of facts and how it comported with the *Weber* criteria, the only difference being that *Weber* had dealt with race and *Johnson* with gender. Both Joyce and Johnson had qualified for the job, and no significant difference in abilities made one clearly better than the other; in such a situation, the employer could legitimately take gender into account.

Woodside also denied that an irreconcilable difference existed between the Seventh and Ninth Circuit decisions. The *Janowiak* case had a completely different set of facts from *Johnson*. In *Janowiak* the district court had issued a summary judgment based on statistics indicating discrimination and had never heard any evidence as to whether there had in fact been any discrimination on the employer's part. The appeals court had reversed because two public task forces had found that despite the statistical imbalance, the employer had never followed any discriminatory policies. Moreover, the Seventh Circuit itself had carefully limited *Janowiak* to its peculiar circumstances, and another more recent decision in the same circuit had been consistent with the Ninth Circuit cases.

The petitioner has a right to file a reply, and Brooks exercised this right. She wanted to emphasize one point, both in terms of securing cert and also as a basis for her later argument. She devoted her reply to one issue, attempting to rebut Woodside's assertion that Joyce and Johnson had been equally well qualified. She quoted extensively from the depositions and the trial to support her claim that Johnson had been far better qualified, and thus the county's plan, in unnecessarily trammeling his rights, had violated the *Weber* standards.

———

When the county's reply had been received, the clerk of the Court distributed it and Johnson's petition to the nine justices. In each chamber, one of the clerks read the two documents and prepared a short summary of the arguments as well as a recommendation whether to grant cert. In late February, Chief Justice Warren E. Burger put No. 85-1129 on the agenda for discussion at the next conference.

For the Supreme Court to grant certiorari, four of the nine justices must agree that there is a case or controversy of sufficient magnitude to warrant the expenditure of the Court's scarce time and resources. The rule of four, as one scholar has noted, "is an intriguing institutional tradition. Four is the perfect number, striking a sensitive balance between principle and pragmatism." If one allowed the chief justice to determine the Court's calendar, that would put too much power in the hands of a person envisioned by the Framers as no more than "first among equals." If five justices had to vote for cert, that would in effect prejudge a case, since the majority could accept only those cases it wished to reverse or affirm for ideological as well as jurisprudential reasons.

Although some of the five-thousand-plus cases reaching the Court each year are frivolous, and most raise no new point of law, many do involve difficult legal and constitutional questions that may require extensive briefing and argument. The rule of four ensures that some of these questions will be heard, and it negates the need to play tough at an early stage of the proceedings. The majority can agree graciously to the wishes of a minority to hear a particular question, recognizing that the minority is only one vote short of a majority. On the other hand, if only two or three people are interested in a case, it will not be heard. For the most part, the rule of four makes sure that insignificant issues will not waste the Court's time and that important questions will usually get onto the calendar.

Prior to the Friday conference, the chief justice will circulate two lists of cases. Special List I, or the Discuss List, includes those petitions for cert that he considers ready and worth discussing. Special List II, the so-called Dead List, contains those petitions he believes not worth discussing, for a variety of reasons, and on which the conference should not waste time. The other justices will have one of their clerks check the list, and if there are no cases that they have a particular interest in, they will agree to deny cert. Discussion will then be confined to just those cases where one or more justices believes significant issues are involved. Ideally, the justices agree to grant or deny cert because of the questions of law involved; in fact, personal views about particular issues will also affect how each justice votes.

At its conference on February 24, 1986, the four most liberal members of the Court, William Brennan, Thurgood Marshall, Harry Blackmun, and John Stevens, voted to deny cert. They had voted to sustain affirmative action plans in prior decisions and saw no reason to disturb the Ninth Circuit's ruling. Justice Louis Powell, the Court's leading centrist, believed that cert should be granted but that the Ninth Circuit decision should then be vacated and the case remanded for review in light of the Court's as yet unannounced decision in No. 84-1340, *Wygant v. Jackson Board of Education*, another affirmative action case. Chief Justice Warren Burger, joined by his three most conservative colleagues, Bryon White, William Rehnquist, and Sandra Day O'Connor, voted to grant cert; the rule of four had been met. The justices agreed that notice that cert had been granted in the *Johnson* case should be held until after the opinion in *Wygant* had been delivered. On July 7, 1986, the U.S. Supreme Court announced that it would hear argument in Paul Johnson's case the following term.

CHAPTER 6

The Changing Law of the Eighties

Steve Woodside walked into 70 West Hedding Street on Monday morning feeling relaxed after enjoying a few days vacation with his family in northern California. He got off the elevator at the ninth floor, and as he walked to his office someone said to him, "Gee, isn't it wonderful about the case?"

"What case?" Steve asked, thinking he had won a suit then pending in a local court.

"The affirmative action case, you know, the one about Diane Joyce. The Supreme Court is going to hear your case."

"Oh, Christ, no, tell me it isn't so," Woodside said, and ran down the hall to his office. There he found his desk piled with letters and telegrams from all over the country, ranging from "You have to settle this case or the Supreme Court will dump affirmative action" to "Boy, we can help you and we can argue the case for you."

To put it mildly, Steve Woodside was not thrilled. Looking back on it later, he said, "Now it's easy to say this is a highlight of my career and all that, but at the time all I could see was a lot of work and a lot of problems. I kept telling myself, 'Keep your mind on your job; your job is to do the best for your clients.' "

Woodside knew that the Court had been split on affirmative action cases and that it could easily reverse the victory he had won in the Ninth Circuit. He looked through a stack of telephone messages and began calling people — Barry Goldstein of the NAACP Inc. Fund and Benna Solomon at the Council of State and Local Governments, asking them what they thought the Court might do. He soon discovered that no consensus existed on either the Court's proclivities or the best way to deal with the issue. Several people suggested that he come to Washington, where they would arrange a meeting of interested groups to discuss strategy. Within a week, Woodside flew east.

In the meantime, he reviewed some of the recent high court cases to see whether the law had changed significantly since the Johnson suit had first begun.

———

Following the *Weber* and *Fullilove* decisions, it had appeared that the Supreme Court would endorse affirmative action as consistent with both Title VII and the Equal Protection Clause. But in the three years since Judge Ingram had first heard Johnson's suit, the high court had decided several other cases that made approval of the Santa Clara plan problematical. Moreover, the Reagan administration in general, and the Justice Department in particular, had declared war on affirmative action, launching one suit after another in efforts to reverse previous settlements and pressuring state and local governments to withdraw from consent decrees that had established preferential hiring programs.

The first case before the Court involved a clash of competing rights, a problem frequently associated with affirmative action programs. In 1980, Memphis, Tennessee, had entered a consent decree following a class action suit initiated by Carl Stotts, a black fireman who charged the city with discrimination in hiring and promotion practices in the fire department. The city agreed to promote certain individuals and established interim goals of filling one-half of job vacancies and 20 percent of promotions in each job category with qualified black applicants. The decree did not contain any provisions for layoffs or for awarding competitive seniority.

The following year, in the face of budget deficits, the city announced that it would have to reduce personnel in nearly all departments and in doing so would follow a "last hired, first fired" rule based on an employee's length of continuous service with the city. Since most black employees had only recently been hired or promoted under the consent decree, nearly all of them — including Carl Stotts — would be let go in the layoff. Stotts went to court and got a temporary restraining order forbidding the layoff of any black employees. The Firefighters Union, which had not been a party to the consent decree but which had negotiated the seniority system with the city, intervened, and then the fight over the seniority system pitted the black firemen against the predominantly white union.

In May 1981, the district court issued a permanent injunction against the city. While it noted that the consent decree had been silent on the question of layoffs, the judge found that the city did not have a bona fide seniority system and therefore could not use seniority as a basis for reducing staff. The Sixth Circuit affirmed the district court's findings, and the union appealed to the Supreme Court. In the meantime, the city's fiscal problems eased, and the white employees laid off had been hired back. The Court could easily have avoided this case by declaring it moot, but at least four justices wanted to deal with the issue, and under the rule of four, the Court granted certiorari.

Justice White handed down the Court's opinion in June 1984, and by a vote of 6 to 3 the justices upheld the vested rights in valid seniority systems against affirmative action plans *(Firefighters Local Union No. 1784 v. Stotts)*. Title VII specifically permitted bona fide seniority plans as justification for differences in compensation and conditions of employment and discharge, and the district court could not ignore the plan in attempting to fashion a remedy against discrimination. Neither the union nor nonminority workers had been parties to the consent decree and therefore had not agreed to give up their rights under the system negotiated with the city.

Chief Justice Burger and Justices Powell and Rehnquist joined White's opinion. Justice Stevens concurred only in the result and thought White's discourse on the meaning of § 703(h) of Title VII, the section on seniority, wholly unnecessary; he would have decided the case on the simple fact that the district court misinterpreted the facts and "abused its discretion."

Justice Sandra Day O'Connor, rapidly becoming a critical centrist vote on affirmative action cases, also concurred with the results but not with the plurality's reasoning. She agreed that a district court could not unilaterally modify a consent decree in a way that impinged on legitimately vested rights, and she pointed out that in their original suit, the black firemen had chosen to ignore the union. They had, she implied, taken the easy way and avoided both the expense of litigation as well as the burden of identifying the specific victims of the city's discriminatory practices. The bargain they struck included the existing seniority system as part of the city's permitted employment practices, and now they had to live with that bargain. O'Connor differed from the majority in that where White implied that no affirmative action plan could take precedence over a bona fide seniority system, O'Connor said that it could if the appropriate steps are taken in the beginning. The process is more difficult, but that is as it should be when competing sets of rights are concerned.

Reagan administration officials were delighted with the *Stotts* ruling. Clarence Pendleton, chairman of the Civil Rights Commission, called the decision a "milestone in . . . limiting the use of so-called remedies such as quotas and similar devices." William Bradford Reynolds, head of the Justice Department's Civil Rights Division and the administration's point man in the war on affirmative action, declared that *Stotts* fully justified the administration's policies. Invoking the case as authority, he called for fifty-one jurisdictions to "cleanse" past consent decrees of anything that even faintly resembled hiring quotas. Union officials, such as Albert Shanker, president of the American Federation of Teachers, praised what he termed "a very important decision" and said that seniority systems, with their built-in objectivity, would in the long run prove beneficial to minorities.

At the other end of the emotional spectrum, civil rights leaders believed the case a disaster. Richard Fields, the attorney for the black firemen, said the decision would allow cities to thwart the gains made through affirmative action. Benjamin Hooks of the NAACP bitterly complained that to uphold the "last hired, first fired" rule "is to turn our backs on the reality that such discriminatory practices have had and continue to have on excluded groups." Judy Goldsmith of the National Organization for Women (NOW) worried that the decision would erode affirmative action as a remedy against race and sex discrimination.

Individuals who stopped to read the opinions carefully noted — correctly — that *Stotts* did not sound the death knell for affirmative action. Linda Greenhouse, the Supreme Court reporter for the *New York Times*, pointed out that the Court traditionally walks a fine line on sensitive issues, avoiding broad-sweeping opinions in favor of narrow rulings on one question at a time. The decision did not break much new ground and did little more than affirm Title VII's explicit protection of seniority systems. Douglas Seaver, a partner in a Boston firm specializing in civil rights and employment law, called the ruling "fairly narrow, and not unexpected." It would require plaintiffs alleging discrimination not only to prove that bias exists, but in securing a remedy, they would have to involve unions representing the non-minority workers and negotiate an arrangement regarding seniority. The real problems, he predicted, would be for union leaders caught between their female and minority members seeking modification of seniority rules and white males demanding full protection of their vested interests.

Some people seemed less worried by the actual decision and more concerned by how the Court had seemingly gone out of its way to reach that decision. At the American Bar Association meeting in Chicago that summer, Justice Stevens, even though he had concurred in the result, strongly criticized his colleagues for their "far-reaching pronouncement" and for "casting aside judicial restraint to move the law to the right." The *New York Times* editorialized that the Court should not have taken *Stotts*, when the issue had already been mooted. Instead, the Court "labored very hard to hand the administration a victory." For a Court that had led the way in the fight against bias, "the decision signals a troublesome retreat." In a similar vein, Vanderbilt law professor Thomas McCoy wondered if *Stotts* would be the first piece in the puzzle, the beginning of the judicial dismantling of affirmative action.

The following term, however, the Court sent contradictory signals on its views of affirmative action. First, it apparently struck a strong blow against preferential hiring plans, and then, in two cases decided at the end of the term, it seemed to reject the broad dicta in White's opinion in *Stotts* and held that under some circumstances race-conscious remedial plans could be instituted that benefited the people who were not the actual victims of discrimination.

In *Wygant v. Jackson Board of Education* (1986), the Court dealt with a situation somewhat different from that of *Stotts*, in that the union had been a party to a collective bargaining agreement incorporating minority protection during layoffs. In 1972, the Jackson, Michigan, school board, in the face of considerable racial tension in the community, negotiated an agreement with the union that in case of layoffs, seniority would be the guiding rule but that the percentage of minority personnel (the last hired) laid off would not exceed the percentage of minorities in the system. The school system, as everyone agreed then and later, had not itself discriminated against minorities, a fact that would become very important to the high court. As a result of the agreement, during two layoffs in 1976 and 1977 and in 1981 and 1982, the school administration retained minority teachers while letting go nonminority faculty with greater seniority. The white teachers sued, not only under Title VII but also under other civil rights statutes as well as the Equal Protection Clause, which established a high level of scrutiny for racial classification.

The district court dismissed the white teachers' claims. With respect to the equal protection claim, the court held that the racial preferences in the collective bargaining agreement did not have to rely on a finding of past particular discrimination. Rather, the school board could use such classifications to provide role models for minority students in an attempt to remedy social discrimination. The Sixth Circuit agreed with this logic, but the Supreme Court did not.

In what had become a familiar pattern, Justice Powell's opinion for the Court had the full endorsement of only the chief justice and Justice Rehnquist, although Justice O'Connor concurred in most of the major points. Justice White gave Powell his fifth vote but concurred only in the result. Justice Marshall dissented, joined by Brennan and Blackmun, while Justice Stevens dissented separately.

Because the challenge invoked equal protection claims, the school plan had to support a "compelling state purpose," and the means chosen had to be narrowly tailored to that purpose. Just as he had in *Bakke*, Powell rejected the notion that "societal discrimination alone is sufficient to justify a legal classification." There had to be proof that the governmental agency involved had engaged in discriminatory practices that it now attempted to remedy. The Jackson school system had no record of prior discrimination, and its plan, to provide role models to counter social bias, struck Powell as vague and far too broad. "Carried to its logical extreme," he wrote, "the idea that black students are better off with black teachers could lead to the very system the Court rejected in *[Brown]*."

Powell went out of his way, however, to acknowledge that "in order to remedy the effects of past discrimination, it may be necessary to take race into account." But such a plan had to be narrowly tailored, in order, among other things, to minimize the burden placed upon innocent nonminority workers. Hiring goals diffuse this burden and impose a lesser hardship than layoffs. "Denial of a future employment opportunity is not as intrusive as loss of an existing job." The Jackson plan, without proof of prior discrimination and an insufficiently narrowly tailored plan, did not meet the strict standards of scrutiny the Court had established for equal protection claims.

During the time the Court had prepared its opinions in *Wygant*, the Reagan administration had made quite clear what it thought the law should be. Attorney General Meese had declared that the very idea of using racial quotas "to remedy the lingering effects of past discrimination is nothing short of a legal and constitutional tragedy." Following announcement of the decision, William Bradford Reynolds claimed a victory for the administration and charged that *Wygant* exposed "a serious constitutional flaw" in the federal government's set-aside requirements. Conservative legal analyst Bruce Fein of the American Enterprise Institute predicted that the ruling would "unravel hundreds of affirmative action plans" across the nation.

Outside the Justice Department, most people did not see *Wygant* as so clear a signal. Paul Gerwitz, professor of civil rights at the Yale Law School, accused Reynolds of "twisting the Court's decision to reach a result that he wants." Barry Goldstein of the Inc. Fund saw the ruling as a victory for civil rights, in that the Court had rejected the Justice Department's argument that only identifiable victims of past discrimination could benefit from remedial plans. A survey of editorial opinion led a major news magazine to headline the article, "Did Court Flash Red, Green or Amber?" It took the title from the *Denver Post*, which charged that the Court had been unable to give either a red or a green light to affirmative action and so had "once again flashed its favorite color: amber."

A few weeks later, just before the Court recessed for the summer, it announced two more affirmative action decisions that muddied the water still further. In *Firefighters v. Cleveland* (1986), Justice Brennan put together a 6-to-3 coalition that gave lower courts broad discretion in fashioning consent decrees that included hiring programs with explicit racial preferences. Brennan distinguished the facts in this case from that of *Stotts* by claiming that the plan in Cleveland, designed to eliminate past patterns of racial discrimination, was a true consent decree, whereas the case in Memphis had arisen from a dispute over modification of a consent decree.

In a far more complicated decision, the Court by a narrow vote upheld a court-ordered goal of 29.23 percent minority membership in a New York union (*Local 28 Sheet Metal Workers v. EEOC* [1986]). The Sheet Metal Workers had originally had a whites-only clause, and even after the state civil rights commission ordered the clause eliminated, it still took no black applicants for membership. The EEOC tried to reason with the union, and when all efforts at mediation failed, the commission, joined by the city and the state, initiated a suit in 1971. In 1977 a federal judge found that not only had the union discriminated, but it also had violated repeated state and federal orders to cease discrimination. He established a nonwhite membership goal of 29 percent, based on the percentage of nonwhites in the relevant local labor pool, and gave the union four years to reach that goal. The union refused to comply, and in 1981 a federal court found Local 28 in contempt of court for its "willful disobedience" and fined it $150,000.

The Supreme Court had no problem with the finding of past discrimination, but did the remedy benefit those who had suffered from that discrimination, or a larger group that included those who were not "identifiable victims"? Justice Brennan, joined by Marshall, Blackmun, and Stevens, upheld the use of explicit racial classification as a remedy for past discrimination, although he conceded that the Court had not agreed "on the proper test to be applied in analyzing the constitutionality of race-conscious measures." Brennan got his majority when Justice Powell concurred in the judgment, agreeing that in some instances goals were necessary. Justice O'Connor concurred in part but dissented from the judgment, believing the court-ordered plan a mandatory quota rather than a goal. White, Rehnquist, and Burger also dissented, on the grounds that the plan not only constituted a quota but benefited those who had not been the victims of discrimination.

Just as civil rights advocates had wept over *Stotts*, they now exulted over these cases. Ralph Neas, the director of the Leadership Conference for Civil Rights, termed the two decisions "a tremendous and historic victory." Barry Goldstein of the NAACP Inc. Fund noted that the Justice Department had wanted to scrap affirmative action altogether; now the Court had ratified affirmative action as an important and legitimate tool in the fight for equality. O. J. Silas, director of affirmative action for Minneapolis, one of the cities under pressure from the Justice Department to annul a consent decree, declared, "It will give us a feeling of not being out there fighting the battle all alone."

Conservatives, on the other hand, took a more pessimistic view. Attorney General Edwin Meese tried to put the best light on the decisions, claiming that even though affirmative action plans had been upheld, the Court had "accepted the general position of this administration that racial preferences are not a good thing to have. What they have done is carve out various exceptions to that general rule, even while affirming the rule itself." Paul Kamenar of the conservative Western Legal Foundation took a far less sanguine view. "It's obviously a defeat for us. If '29.23 percent' isn't a quota, I'd like to know what is."

In fact, the decisions in these cases did not mark any significant shift in the Court one way or the other but mirrored the lack of consensus within it. To begin with, the justices split deeply in all the opinions, with no five members endorsing any particular point of view. A majority did, however, firmly reject the Reagan administration's view that court-ordered racial preferences in hiring and promotion were illegal, except to benefit those victims who had personally suffered discrimination. On the other hand, a somewhat different majority agreed that judges should impose affirmative action with racial quotas only as a last-ditch remedy for "egregious" discrimination, the kind encountered in the sheetmetal workers union. In an analysis of *Wygant*, which applied equally well to the Court's entire collection of affirmative action decisions, Daniel Seligman wrote:

> We still cannot figure out when it is naughty to reverse-discriminate and when it is nice. There now seems to be absolutely nobody under those robes willing to just haul off and say you can't discriminate. So the forecast here is for additional decades of ontological hairsplitting over the difference between a "compelling" governmental interest and one that is merely "important."

———

The Court during these years had also handed down some additional opinions regarding gender discrimination in employment, and although none of these involved affirmative action plans, they signaled the importance the Court attached to this issue. In 1981 the Court, by a 5-to-4 vote, held that women could file certain claims alleging sex-based wage discrimination under Title VII, even if no man held an equal but higher paying job (*County of Washington v. Gunther* [1981]). The issue revolved around the interaction of the Equal Pay Act of 1963, which did not apply to municipal and state employees until 1974, and the Bennett Amendment, §703(h), to Title VII, adopted at the time of its passage in 1964. The section incorporated the so-called "affirmative defenses" of the earlier act, in which employers could support sex-based wage differentials because of seniority, merit, quantity or quality of production, or "any other factor other than sex."

Female prison guards in Washington County, Oregon, made substantially less than their male counterparts; in 1973, the monthly pay scale for female guards ranged from $476 to $606; male guards earned from $668 to $853. The county argued that the male guards supervised ten times as many prisoners per guard as did the women, who spent much of their time doing less valuable clerical work. On this basis, the district court dismissed the suit by the female guards. While the court of appeals agreed that on the basis of work alone the county did not have to pay the women the same as the men, it nonetheless held that Title VII permitted wage discrimination suits, even if the women's jobs were not equal to those of the higher paid males, if it could be shown that the lower wages resulted at least in part from intentional discrimination.

The high court agreed, and Justice Brennan emphasized the narrow question before the Court. The Equal Pay Act had resolved the issue of equal pay for equal work, so that if the women guards performed the same tasks as the men and supervised roughly the same number of prisoners, any wage differential would be illegal. Here the county had proved that the men and women had different levels of responsibility, which would justify some of the discrepancy in wage rates. If women could prove that sex discrimination accounted for at least part of the differential, then they could sue under Title VII. Thus, women could go beyond the straightforward equal pay for equal work standard and seek redress even if one of the affirmative defenses existed, provided they could offer proof of gender discrimination.

In 1983, the Court decided two cases affecting gender discrimination in employment. In the *Manhart* decision in 1978, the Court had held that, despite actuarial tables showing that women as a class lived longer than men, employers could not require women to make larger contributions to a retirement plan and then receive the same monthly payments as men. In *Arizona Governing Committee v. Norris*, a closely divided Court held that if men and women had paid the same retirement premiums, they could not be paid lesser monthly benefits.

In another case that term, the Court held that employers had to provide the same medical coverage for pregnancy in the benefits plan offered to male as to female employees. In 1976, the Court had ruled that Title VII did not prohibit gender discrimination based on pregnancy, and two years later Congress amended the law explicitly to prohibit such discrimination. An employer immediately changed its health insurance package to provide better pregnancy coverage to its female workers but did not provide the same level of coverage in its family plan to the wives of male workers. Some male employees filed a gender discrimination suit, and Justice Stevens, speaking for a 7-to-2 majority, upheld the EEOC determination that the amendment required equal health care packages (*Newport News Shipbuilding & Dry Dock Co. v. EEOC*).

In its next term, the Court handed down a unanimous decision in a well-publicized case involving discrimination against women in law firms. Following her graduation from law school, Elizabeth Hishon had accepted a position with the large Atlanta firm of King & Spalding, assuming that if she performed well, she would, like her male associates, be made a partner. In 1978 and again in 1979 the firm passed her over for partnership, and she had to leave the firm. At the time, King & Spalding had fifty partners and fifty associates, but not a single female partner. Hishon went to the EEOC, claiming that she had been discriminated against on the basis of her sex in violation of Title VII, and the commission issued a right to sue letter. The lower courts dismissed her suit, however, on the grounds that Title VII did not apply to the selection of partners by a partnership.

Chief Justice Burger spoke for the entire bench in rejecting the law firm's contention that as a partnership it did not come within the reach of Title VII. Modern large law firms differed significantly from nineteenth- and early twentieth-century arrangements involving only a handful of lawyers. Modern firms had dozens, perhaps hundreds of attorneys, with associates on a salaried basis, as well as many more people in support positions, and as such qualified as employers within the definition of Title VII. When hiring new associates, the assumption that good work would ultimately be rewarded by partnership constituted part and parcel of the contractual relationship. Gender could not be the grounds for withholding partnership, and discrimination on that basis would violate Title VII (*Hishon v. King & Spaulding* [1984]).

The final days of the Burger Court brought another decision that cheered feminists both by its holding and by the near-unanimity of the justices. William Rehnquist, whom many women believed the justice least sympathetic to feminist claims, spoke for the Court in holding that sexual harassment constituted sex discrimination under Title VII. The law not only forbade the demand of sexual favors as a quid pro quo for hiring or promotion but also reached situations in which harassment had created an abusive work environment.

Sidney Taylor, a vice-president of a bank and manager of one of its branches, had hired Michelle Vinson as a teller. Four years later, by which time Vinson had advanced to assistant branch manager, the bank discharged her for excessive use of sick leave. She then brought suit charging that she had been sexually harassed by Taylor and that she had agreed to sleep with him out of fear of losing her job. The bank had responded that no grounds for a suit existed and that because Vinson had voluntarily agreed to Taylor's advances, there had been no harassment. It also introduced evidence about Vinson's dress and personal fantasies to buttress its claim that the woman had voluntarily become Taylor's sex partner.

Rehnquist's opinion for a unanimous Court displayed a great sensitivity to the first issue and to the psychological pressures on employees told that their advancement rested on submitting to unwanted sexual advances. The district court had ruled that because of the "voluntary" nature of the sexual conduct, Vinson had had no grounds for a suit. Rehnquist rejected this view and announced that "the correct inquiry is whether respondent by her conduct indicated that the alleged sexual advances were unwelcome, not whether her actual participation in sexual intercourse was voluntary" (*Meritor Savings Bank v. Vinson* [1986]).

The Court did, however, agree that the evidence regarding Vinson's dress and alleged fantasies might be admitted and would depend upon the judge's evaluation of whether it would be relevant or prejudicial to the case. This ruling angered a number of feminists, who wondered what relevance a woman's private dreams would have in a harassment case. Leaving the issue of admissibility up to individual judges, Wendy Williams charged, recalled the days when a woman's sexual history had been deemed "obviously relevant" as to whether or not she "voluntarily" consented to intercourse with an accused rapist.

Looking at the law that would govern the *Johnson* case in summer 1986, one could not predict which way the Supreme Court would go. Attorneys on both sides believed that they could win, but only by a close vote. In terms of affirmative action, the Court since *Weber* had upheld that idea, especially in circumstances where the record showed a clear pattern of past discrimination. But when preferential hiring plans came up against other rights, such as seniority, the Court had been less sympathetic. On the other hand, the Burger Court had taken the lead in moving women out of the legal dark ages, and a clear majority on the Court viewed Title VII as a distinct barrier to gender discrimination.

The Burger Court, however, would not be hearing the case. A few days before the end of the 1985 term, Warren Burger announced his retirement from the center chair. President Reagan promptly named William H. Rehnquist, the Court's most conservative member, to be the sixteenth chief justice of the United States. To take Rehnquist's seat as associate justice, the president nominated Antonin Scalia, a member of the court of appeals for the District of Columbia and widely recognized as a brilliant and very conservative jurist. The addition of Scalia and Burger's departure would not affect the general lineup of the Court, but the trio of Rehnquist, O'Connor, and Scalia would provide a conservative bloc that, for the first time in years, could supply a cohesive jurisprudential rationale for moving the Court to the right.

CHAPTER 7

Preparing for Battle

Arguing a case before the U.S. Supreme Court is a daunting proposition, even for experienced trial lawyers. A Daniel Webster, a Felix Frankfurter, or an Abe Fortas may feel comfortable at the lectern, but for most attorneys, the thirty minutes or so they have to present their argument may well prove the most frightening, as well as the most exhilarating, thirty minutes of their professional career.

Between the time that the Court grants certiorari and when it actually hears a case, the attorneys must meet certain requirements established by the Court, both in terms of their own qualifications as well as the written materials they would submit. Both sides have to plot a strategy and contingency plans, should the justices decide to pursue particular issues. Negotiations have to be conducted with each other and with interested parties who file *amicus* briefs. And, as the tension mounts until the clerk sets the argument date and the Court actually hears the case, one has to look after the client's best interests, which means following other cases and business for one's employers.

Neither Steve Woodside nor Connie Brooks had yet applied for admission to the Supreme Court bar, a qualification necessary to practice before the nation's highest court. The Supreme Court bar has thousands of members, the vast majority of whom join for the cachet of hanging the certificate on their office walls. Others join in the hope that someday they may indeed have a case to argue at the marble palace, or, if they are members of the solicitor general's office, because they can reasonably expect to represent the government before the Court. When lightning does strike and an attorney suddenly learns that cert has been granted, he or she can then send the application form and a check for $100 to the clerk of the Court. There is no examination; one need only be a member in good standing of a state bar and have had five years experience as a practicing attorney.

At Mountain States, with its limited budget and small staff of young lawyers, most of them only a few years out of law school, Connie Brooks clearly would argue the case. Santa Clara County, on the other hand, had the resources to hire an outside attorney, but the Board of Supervisors had faith in Steve Woodside. He had, after all, argued successfully in the Fourth Circuit, and he knew the record in a way that no one coming in at this date could hope to match. So the board, which had now become very interested in the case, expressed its confidence in their staff attorney and authorized him to secure outside help to assist him in his preparation.

Other people, however, did not know Woodside or share the board's confidence, a situation that became apparent at the meeting in Washington in early August 1986. Representatives from a number of civil rights groups gathered to discuss the implications of *Johnson* and another affirmative action case scheduled to be argued around the same time, *United States v. Paradise*. On the way to Washington Woodside had decided that these people needed above all else a clear statement of the facts in the case, an account similar to the one he would prepare as part of his brief.

At the meeting Woodside sensed that many of the participants looked somewhat askance at him. With a parochialism typical of many East Coasters, they saw a boyish assistant counsel from what they considered a little California town. He had never been before the Supreme Court before. He worked for a local agency and therefore did not see himself as a plaintiff's attorney pursuing civil rights goals. He had limited Title VII experience. Without actually saying so, many of them indicated that they thought he would lose.

They were smart enough, however, to recognize that as the named respondent in the suit, Santa Clara County could choose whichever lawyer it wanted. So they held back expressing their reservations and began to ask serious and difficult questions about the case, especially about the Ninth Circuit opinion, which they thought absolutely terrible.

Woodside, in turn, went out of his way to show them that he knew the case. "In addition to what you're hearing about the Ninth Circuit," he said, "there are other facts relevant to this case, including

Diane Joyce being denied opportunities earlier in her career." Moreover, his client would still prefer to reach an agreement with Paul Johnson and moot the case, thus shielding its affirmative action plan from a possible invalidation by the high court. Finally, Woodside wanted them to know that he felt competent and confident about handling the case. "I'm not an expert in this field of law," he conceded, "but I know enough about it to think that the Court is divided, that there are some key swing votes, namely O'Connor and Powell, and I think I can convince."

Woodside's candor won over some of the skeptics; the rest, whatever their private feelings, realized that he had no intention of giving up control of the case. So they offered him their help, some of which proved quite valuable later on, and he in turn agreed that some of the organizations there ought to enter *amicus* briefs in support of the county plan. Feeling that he had hurdled a considerable barrier, Woodside returned to San Jose to begin serious preparation of his brief.

———

One reason that there are so few unanimous decisions in the Supreme Court is that it takes only difficult cases that raise new or complex issues of law or both. If the question is simple, the lower courts should have had no difficulty in answering it correctly; when the lower courts differ, or where at least four of the justices question whether the lower courts got it right, then the nation's highest tribunal will hear the case.

At the beginning of a suit, in the original trial phase, the burden of evidence is on the party bringing the complaint. In this case, Paul Johnson, through his attorney, had had the burden of proving to Judge Ingram that the county had discriminated against him. The defendant, in turn, has no burden unless and until the plaintiff can make a reasonable case that discrimination did occur, and then it has the burden of rebuttal.

At the court of appeals, the burden is on the petitioner, the party that has lost and is appealing the lower court's decision. Counsel has to make the oftentimes difficult argument that the trial judge misinterpreted the law; the winning party has the easier time in that he or she is telling the court, "Look, one of your fellow judges decided it this way, and that judge knows the law, so the decision should be left alone."

In the Supreme Court, one might expect that there would be a similar burden on the petitioner, a greater barrier to hurdle than that facing the party who won in the lower court. This situation holds when one party is seeking to overturn a long line of precedents and to have the Court announce a radical departure in the law. That burden, however, comes not from saying that the lower courts made a wrong decision but from arguing that the honorable justices of the Supreme Court of the United States made an error. Precedent is a powerful conservative force, but the Court has on a number of occasions admitted that it had been wrong in the past, on issues such as racial segregation, the right to counsel, and legislative apportionment. Otherwise the very difficulty of the cases confronting the Court tend to place both parties on a more or less equal basis. In new questions, the Court is not bound by its own prior rulings on the issue, and very often, there is a difference among the circuits, so both sides have to argue that at least one of the courts of appeals decided incorrectly. In some ways, there is a slight advantage to the petitioner. Having lost below, this is the last chance, so counsel can risk pursuing a more aggressive line of argument; the respondent is confined to the more conservative stance of defending the opinion of the lower court, no matter how weak or poorly reasoned it may be.

In deciding cases before it, the Supreme Court relies on the written briefs and responses to determine the relevant facts and law about a case. There is a great deal of debate over whether or not oral argument affects how the justices vote, but there is no question that a poor brief will work against a litigant's position. Under the rules of the Court, each side must present a brief that follows a set format and that does not exceed fifty pages. First comes the central question or questions in the case, followed by a table of authorities, a narrative of the case, a summary of the argument, and then the argument itself, with the main points set off in different typeface. The petitioner's briefs and replies must be bound in blue, those of the respondent in red. Both sides agree to a so-called "joint appendix," which includes relevant evidence from earlier stages in the suit, such as copies of exhibits, excerpts from the trial transcript, and affidavits. The joint appendix for this case included docket entries for the district and appeals courts, the original complaint made by Johnson, the EEOC right-to-sue letter, the county's answer to the complaint, the joint pretrial statement, exhibits from the trial illustrating the county's notice of positions and its affirmative action plan, and an affidavit by Kristina Sermersheim. The joint appendix provides the record the justices will use in reviewing the case.

Both sides also have a great deal of law on which to rely, and in the briefs they present — in as strong a manner as possible — what they believe to be the correct interpretation. In the brief for Paul Johnson, Connie Brooks elected a strategy of focusing on a single question and phrased that question in a way which, if the Court adopted it, would make it impossible to rule for the county:

> May a public employer lawfully promote a less-qualified female candidate over a more-qualified male employee allegedly pursuant to an affirmative action plan adopted solely to eliminate a statistical disparity in the work force, unrelated to sex discrimination?

By wording it this way, Brooks reminded the Court that in prior decisions it had held that employers, for the sake of affirmative action, did not have to hire or promote less qualified minority applicants. By claiming that the statistical disparity had no relationship to gender discrimination, she referred to the several cases in which there had been a finding of prior discrimination as a necessary predicate for an affirmative action plan. She was arguing that the law cannot possibly mean that an employer can discriminate against a well-qualified white male when there had never been any bias against women and minorities. Her legal arguments buttressed this line of reasoning:

- The agency plan lacked any remedial justification because the agency had never been guilty of sexual discrimination. Moreover, according to the Court's recent decision in *Wygant*, one could not adopt affirmative action in response to alleged general social discrimination.
- Even if there had been a legitimate remedial purpose, the plan failed because it had not been narrowly tailored so as to avoid unnecessarily trammeling the rights of white males such as Paul Johnson.
- *Weber*, which involved a private employer, did not apply to a public employer, but even if it did, the agency plan did not meet the *Weber* guidelines.

- Because the county had admitted that Johnson had been denied promotion solely on the basis of his sex, the county had to bear the burden of proof to show that it had not violated his Title VII rights. In other words, the county had to prove the necessity and appropriateness of the affirmative action plan; Paul Johnson did not have the burden of proving its inappropriateness.

In each assertion, Brooks singled out the very points of law that had become the norm in suits challenging affirmative action plans, questions concerning the remedial nature of the plan, its scope of operation, the factual situation that made it necessary, and the evidentiary criteria applicable in such cases. But with *Wygant* so recently decided, she also tried to hook in a new argument that had until this point been absent from the case — the equal protection claim that would have shifted the focus of the case from a question of statutory interpretation (did Title VII permit such a plan) to that of whether the plan violated the Constitution — and thus invoked a much higher level of scrutiny and a much greater burden on the county to justify its plan.

A voluntary affirmative action plan by a public employer must be reviewed under the Fourteenth Amendment's strict scrutiny standard even though the Petitioner only claims violation under Title VII. . . . Even though this case concerns a sex-based classification, it should be subject to strict scrutiny because neither Title VII nor the Fourteenth Amendment countenance discrimination and any exception to that principle established by this Court should be very narrow.

Here Brooks invited the Court to take a major step in employment discrimination jurisprudence, elevate sex to the same level as race, and impose the same strict scrutiny standard on any plan designed to alleviate alleged gender bias as it applied to racial classification. This question had been raised before the Court in previous cases, and a majority had never been willing to go that far.

In order to take that step, however, the Court also had to accept constitutional claims raised under the Equal Protection Clause, and those claims had not been raised in this particular case. Johnson had won on Title VII in the district court, and the court of appeals, in overturning that judgment, had also limited itself to Title VII questions. It had been Jim Dawson's strategy from the start to go with Title VII rather than with constitutional claims because Title VII law in 1981 seemed much clearer on the subject. At the time, *Bakke* and *Weber* had been the controlling cases, not *Wygant*, and now Brooks wanted the justices to inject a new issue, one that had not been litigated in the lower courts. If they accepted her invitation, Paul Johnson had a good chance of winning.

———

Brooks had contacted Rex Lee, the former solicitor general of the United States and a leading conservative, right after cert had been granted and asked for his assistance. In the fairly short turn-around time they had had to prepare the brief, he had been one of the people to critique it; he also put Brooks in touch with people in the Justice Department who could provide information and assistance. She had known Lee for a number of years, and his knowledge of and experience with the Court would prove useful.

After filing her brief, Brooks began to prepare for oral argument. She had never considered herself as a civil rights expert, so she had to be sure that at the least she knew the major recent cases in that area. An associate at Mountain States, Diane Vaksdal, had worked on preparing the *Wygant* case and had also helped Brooks write the *Johnson* brief. Vaksdal put together a briefing book consisting of the major statutes and decisions of the last ten years. "Here it is," she said, and handed the thick binder to Brooks. "Learn it." Brooks did. As part of her preparation, she outlined in detail every one of the Supreme Court's civil rights decisions in the past decade. She wanted to see not only what key issues had been common to several cases but also how the individual justices responded to these questions. And she had to master the record in Paul Johnson's case. Though she might never have as intimate a knowledge as Steve Woodside, she had to know the material so that she would not make a factual error in responding to a question from the bench.

In preparing her argument, Brooks followed a pattern she had used in other cases — make the points so clear that her mother (the archetypical layperson) would understand them. While the law can often be complex and obtuse, one mark of a good lawyer is the ability to state the legal issues clearly and succinctly, a talent prized by judges as much as juries. Loading up her argument with extensive quotes and citations would not be effective.

Brooks knew that of the thirty minutes assigned to her argument, she would be lucky if she had five minutes to make the statement of her case, with the rest of her time spent answering questions. So she wrote out fairly lengthy narratives and then boiled them down as much as possible. This way, she hoped, she would be able to get back on track quickly after a question. Her husband, Vaksdal, and other people helping her wrote down questions they thought the justices would ask, so she could have answers ready; as it turned out, every question from the bench had been anticipated in these sessions.

Like Steve Woodside, Connie Brooks had had a great deal of experience in the lower courts, but the Supreme Court would be different. To help her prepare for the hearing, the Justice Department set up a moot court where she could practice her argument and respond to questions. A moot court is a mock trial, in which real issues are argued before stand-in judges. In law school, students are assigned sides in a case and get their first experience arguing before a jury of other students or a panel of judges drawn from the faculty. For this panel, scheduled a few days before the Court hearing, the leading lawyers in the Civil Rights Department, including William Bradford Reynolds, peppered her with questions and critiqued her responses. She felt ready — scared, but ready.

———

Down in San Jose, Steve Woodside went through his own preparations for battle, and like Brooks, had no hesitation in bringing in some outside experts on the Supreme Court. One of the most knowledgeable Title VII attorneys on the West Coast, Morris Baller, helped with the brief, offering suggestions and editing drafts. Russell Galloway of the University of Santa Clara Law School had recently spent a year observing oral arguments in the Court and had a clear view of the different styles and interests of each justice. Edward Steinman, another member of the Santa Clara faculty, had argued a half-dozen cases in the Supreme Court, and Woodside spent a lot of time with him trying to get a feel for what, at best, would be an unpredictable experience.

The respondent's brief is, at least in part, a response to that of the petitioner, and once the county had received a copy of the Mountain States brief, it had thirty days to complete two tasks — rebut the petitioner's claims of law and fact and put forward its own interpretations. Woodside used the same question he had employed in his earlier brief responding to Johnson's petition for cert, emphasizing that the county plan, with no quotas or rigid preferences, took gender as one consideration in promoting a fully qualified person into a job category that had hitherto not had any women. In his narrative of the facts, he also emphasized that Diane Joyce had qualified for the job and that under the county's accepted personnel procedures, she had been considered as well qualified for the position as Paul Johnson.

The county's argument had two points. Just as Brooks had rung changes on most of the arguments made against affirmative action, Woodside lined up the traditional arguments in favor. He spent nearly thirty pages demonstrating that the county plan met the *Weber* criteria. The county had a firm basis to believe a plan necessary; the facts supported the county's conclusion to initiate a remedial program; that plan had been narrowly tailored to meet its objectives; and the decision to promote a fully qualified woman did not violate the petitioner's Title VII rights.

In his second point, Woodside argued that the Court should reject Brooks's "belated" effort to ground her case on the Equal Protection Clause. That claim had not been raised in the lower courts, but even if it had, the county's plan would have met the test.

Local 715, which had intervened in the case following Judge Ingram's decision, was also a respondent in the case, and David Rosenfeld filed a separate brief. While he concurred in the major points put forward by the county, the union attorney wanted to emphasize that the facts, even without a formal finding of discrimination, justified both the affirmative action plan as well as Diane Joyce's promotion. The union had been a prime mover in getting the plan adopted, and it wanted to drive home the fact that sufficient evidence existed to warrant what the county, and the union, had done.

Once the briefs had been submitted, Woodside began his preparation for the oral argument by participating in several moot courts, both in California and later in Washington. Woodside had experience both in bench and jury trials and before three-judge panels in the

Ninth Circuit. But how did one handle a panel of nine judges? Would it be possible to look at all of them at the same time? (It would not!) How did one retreat, with a minimum of damage, from hostile questioning?

David Rosenfeld helped set up some moot courts in the Bay Area, with participants who knew Title VII law and who could pepper Woodside with the type of questioning he would face in the Supreme Court. In October, Woodside flew to Washington to watch an old friend and colleague, Mary Johnson, argue her first case in the Supreme Court. He had never been in the Marble Palace, so he took a tour of the courtroom and the library as part of a plan to feel at home on November 12, the day the Court had set for the oral argument.

———

In addition to briefs from the litigants, the Supreme Court will also accept written arguments from other parties who have a strong interest in the results of the case. In some instances, such as the desegregation cases, the Court may ask the attorneys general of some states to file *amicus curiae*, or "friend of the court" briefs. The more likely situation is that different interest groups, recognizing the importance of the case, will file briefs presenting their particular views; the more important or controversial the issue, the greater number of *amicus* briefs the Court is likely to receive. When it heard the *Bakke* case in 1978, 120 organizations signed fifty-eight *amicus* briefs; eighty-three supported the position of the University of California, thirty-two supported Bakke, and five urged the Court not to accept the case.

In *Johnson v. Transportation Agency*, forty groups entered eight *amicus* briefs supporting the county and the idea of affirmative action: the National League of Cities, together with the National Association of Counties, the U.S. Conference of Mayors, and the International City Management Association; the City of Detroit, with the District of Columbia and the City of Los Angeles; the Equal Employment Advisory Council; the Lawyers' Committee for Civil Rights Under Law, together with the Mexican-American Legal Defense and Education Fund, the NAACP, and the Puerto Rican Legal Defense and Education Fund; the National Organization for Women Legal Defense and Education Fund, joined by NOW, the ACLU, California Women Lawyers, the Employment Law Center, Equal

Rights Advocates, Federally Employed Women Legal and Educational Fund, the League of Women Voters of the United States, the NAACP Legal Defense and Educational Fund, the National Women's Law Center, Women Employed, Women's Equity Action League, the Women's Law Project, and the Women's Legal Defense Fund; the State of California and the California Fair Employment and Housing Commission, joined by the states of Idaho, Louisiana, Maryland, Michigan, Minnesota, Nebraska, New York, Oregon, Wisconsin, and the Pennsylvania Human Relations Commission; the AFL–CIO; and the American Society for Personnel Administration. Only two public interest groups, the Mid-Atlantic Legal Foundation and the Pacific Legal Foundation, entered *amicus* briefs in support of Johnson.

Generally, the *amicus* briefs presented essentially the same legal arguments as could be found in the principal briefs, although slanted to make the point in a way that related to the group's interests. The National Organization for Women, for example, emphasized the discrimination faced by females in entering traditionally male job markets and pointed out that once the barrier has been breached, women did indeed want to work at those jobs. The AFL–CIO differed somewhat with Local 715 and the county in its interpretation of what *Weber* required as proof of prior discrimination to establish an affirmative action plan. The AFL–CIO wanted *Weber* read liberally, so that employers and unions could have wide latitude in their efforts to remedy past subtle as well as overt discrimination.

The employer groups supporting the respondent, including the states, operated some affirmative action plans under their aegis, and whether private employer or public, wanted the idea of affirmative action upheld. To have struck down the Santa Clara plan would have called into question nearly every public preferential hiring plan in the nation. That, of course, is exactly what the Reagan administration wanted, and it had its say in this case in the *amicus* brief submitted by the solicitor general, Charles Fried.

———

The solicitor general's office in the Justice Department, ever since the creation of the position in 1870, has been responsible for representing the federal government in court, and especially in the Supreme

Court. From the Court's viewpoint, the office performs some valuable work. It screens all potential appeals and petitions in which the government is involved and decides which should be taken to the Court. Although the justices will not automatically grant cert to every petition filed by the solicitor general, the fact that he has screened out a large number does make them more sympathetic to the ones that are filed. Between 1977 and 1981, the Court granted review in 70 percent of the cases filed by the government but in only 6 percent of all other cases.

Whenever the Supreme Court grants cert, it automatically sends a copy of the petitions to the Justice Department to see if the government has an interest in the issue of a sufficient degree to warrant its participation, either as an *amicus* or in cooperation with one of the litigants. The briefs are routed to the division that has responsibility, and it in turn sends a report to the solicitor general, who makes the final determination of whether to get involved. In Paul Johnson's case, the briefs had gone to the Civil Rights Division, which, under William Bradford Reynolds, opposed any affirmative action plan that involved quotas and that did not result from a clear pattern of prior discrimination. The division recommended that the federal government join Johnson's case; the final decision would be up to the solicitor general.

While the Justice Department always has the right to submit an *amicus* brief, the solicitor general does not have an automatic right to participate in oral argument. Each side is normally given thirty minutes for oral argument, and if a litigant wants to have the solicitor general speak on his or her side, that time is deducted from their thirty minutes. Fried very much wanted to appear before the Court in *Johnson*; ever since he had joined the Justice Department a year earlier, he had strenuously opposed preferential hiring plans. At a banquet in honor of William Bradford Reynolds, Fried sounded the clarion call of the Reagan administration:

By 1980, this country was in danger of becoming a quota society. By 1980, we were in danger of a situation with jobs — private and public sector — educational opportunities, housing, judgeships — all the good things were being handed out, not on merit, but by a racial and ethnic and religious and gender spoils system. The

American people elected Ronald Reagan to restore the idea of equality of opportunity and the great ideal of the unity of all mankind. Today that danger is further from us than it was in 1980. And if Ronald Reagan has been able to keep his promise, it is largely because of the work of Brad Reynolds.

Fried had pressed the administration view in a number of cases, with only minimal success, and by the time the *Johnson* brief came across his desk, he had recognized that only a more moderate position could hope to win judicial approval. The hardline conservatives would permit only victim-specific remedies; if a particular black or woman or Hispanic could prove that he or she had been discriminated against, then the courts could order a hiring or promotion to make that particular person whole. Paul Johnson had essentially done this at the district court level; he had proven to the judge that he had been the victim of discrimination, and the court had ordered the county to promote him and pay him the differential in wages. If a black or a woman could make the case, then they should be helped. But plans addressed to groups or to remedy social discrimination did no more than substitute one bias for another.

Fried also opposed quotas but would have allowed a preferential hiring plan for groups if there had been actual discrimination against that group. If an employer could be shown to have deliberately refused to hire or promote blacks, that would be the factual basis for justifying a limited affirmative action plan, one narrowly tailored to address this particular situation.

But he saw no factual predicate in Santa Clara County. The fact that there had been no women on road crews did not, by itself, prove discrimination; one would have to show that the employer had erected barriers against women. "If there are no barriers, then there's no discrimination," he said. "Just because you think it would be nice to have a certain representation of women, what I call the United Nations model, that is not enough reason to prefer a woman over a man, a black over a white."

The problem, as Fried saw it, centered on how one established that discrimination really existed. Did statistics showing a disproportionate lack of a particular group in certain jobs prove discrimination? Or did the numbers themselves constitute the sin, that is, it is terrible that there are none or only a few blacks, women, Hispanics in these jobs, regardless of whether the employer had deliberately kept them out or if other, possibly benign, factors had been at work. *Johnson* seemed an ideal case in which Fried could make this argument.

Connie Brooks, on the other hand, believed the liabilities of having Fried appear far outweighed any possible benefits. The government had just recently lost the two major civil rights cases of the 1985 term, the Cleveland firefighters suit and the New York sheetmetal workers decision. These had been two high profile cases that, according to Brooks, Charles Fried had not only lost, but the Court had in each instance handed down opinions highly critical of the government's position. Along with Reynolds, Fried had emerged as the palladin of the Reagan administration's efforts to undo thirty years of civil rights progress, progress that the Justice Department had previously championed, a situation that the plurality opinions in several cases had commented upon critically. Brooks wanted to find a middle ground on which at least five justices could agree; Fried, in her opinion, would only polarize the Court. She also knew that the year before, Mountain States had turned down Fried's request to share time in *Wygant*, and that apparently had been the proper strategy.

Upon learning of Brooks's decision, a piqued solicitor general tried to force the young woman to change her mind. He called his good friend Rex Lee to ask him to intercede. Brooks received phone calls late at night and early in the morning from conservative groups pressuring her to let Fried join in the oral argument. She in turn talked to a lot of people she knew in Washington, and nearly all of them told her the same thing—keep Charles Fried out! A federal appeals judge whom she knew told her that she could cross Justice Stevens's vote off if Fried appeared. Though she agonized over the decision, in the end she kept to it, and Fried had to be content with filing an *amicus* brief.

The solicitor general argued one main point in the brief, that the county had failed to justify its discriminatory actions against Johnson because its affirmative action plan did not result from a clear record of prior discrimination. Moreover, even legitimate affirmative action plans had to be narrowly tailored in order to protect the interests of innocent persons. But Fried did not claim that there had been absolutely no prior discrimination; rather, he suggested, the issue had not been investigated properly by the lower courts.

This ploy would give the justices, if they wanted it, an opportunity to remand the case to the district court for a new hearing to determine if, in fact, the numerical disparities actually showed prior discrimination. A remand would be a victory for the government, because it would seem to support the Reagan administration's view of affirmative action, and nearly everyone admitted that whatever the numbers, the county had never committed deliberate discrimination. Moreover, a new trial would have to take account of *Wygant* and introduce the higher standards of equal protection into the equation.

———

A few days before the hearing, Woodside flew back to Washington, accompanied by his colleague from the county counsel's office, Ann Ravel. (Dave Rosenfeld, who had wanted to have part of the oral argument, had tried unsuccessfully to have the union pressure the county into this arrangement. He decided to stay in San Francisco and not "waste his client's money" on a useless trip.) Suzanne Wilson and Zoe Lofgren from the Board of Supervisors came to hear the case, and they arranged for Diane Joyce and her pregnant daughter, Donna, to be there as well. Kristy Sermersheim, still assigned to support Joyce, represented the union.

On Tuesday, November 11, Woodside went through one last moot court arranged by the League of Cities. The league had a fairly sophisticated arrangement, with videotape facilities and a panel made up of former Supreme Court law clerks, each of whom would ask the type of questions that one might expect from their respective judges. This last session went well, with only one hitch. At the start of the hearing, each attorney stands up and identifies himself or herself to the Court and whom they are representing. In the practice session at the League of Cities, Woodside had said he represented the respondents, Santa Clara County and Local 715 of the Service Employees International Union. Several of the critics immediately urged him not to say that. "Don't rub it in that you're here for the union to Justice Scalia, or to these other folks," they warned. "Just say you're here for the county."

Woodside went over to confer with Kristy Sermersheim and Diane Joyce. "They're telling us that I need to not say that we're here together. Is that okay? It's really up to you."

Sermersheim later recalled how much this idea frightened her. She thought, "If we don't get credit for this, there goes all the work we've done. But if Diane loses, this would be awful, too." She and Diane spoke together for a few minutes, and then she told Steve, "Just go ahead and win it."

Steve nodded and returned to the practice session. "May it please the Court, my name is Steven Woodside, and I represent the respondent, Transportation Agency of Santa Clara County, California." After the session, he went back to his hotel to rest and to wait. A few blocks away, Connie Brooks did the same.

CHAPTER 8

Before the Bar

At 10:00 on Wednesday morning, November 12, 1986, the marshal of the Supreme Court of the United States, formally dressed, as always, stood and called out, "All rise!" As the audience clambered to their feet, the nine members of the nation's highest tribunal filed in through the red velvet curtain in back of the bench and stood behind their chairs as the marshal called out the traditional opening.

"Oyez, oyez, oyez. The honorable, the chief justice and the associate justices of the Supreme Court of the United States. All persons having business before the honorable, the Supreme Court of the United States, are admonished to draw near and give their attention, for the Court is now sitting. God save the United States and this honorable court."

The months and years of litigation, of planning and research, now came to fruition. The Court had allotted one hour for oral argument and then would take the case under advisement. If Paul Johnson lost here, he had no other legal avenues to pursue; even if he did not lose, he might not necessarily win. Rather than affirming or striking down the Santa Clara plan, the justices might take the advice of the solicitor general and remand to the district court with orders to rehear the suit. In that case, it would be starting over at square one.

Johnson and his wife Betty had come to Washington to hear the case argued. So had Diane Joyce, who, along with her daughter, Donna, had come as guests of the county. This was the first time they had been in the marble palace, and they looked carefully at the eight men and one woman, clad in black robes, who now settled down in their large chairs to hear the case. Connie Brooks and Jim Dawson, sitting at the petitioner's counsel table, and Steve Woodside and Ann Ravel, at the respondent's table, also studied the people sitting at the slightly curved and elevated bench before them. They thought it too close to call, and both sides expected that, whoever won, it would be by a 5-to-4 vote.

―――――

By tradition, the justices sit according to their seniority on the Court, with the chief justice in the middle, the most senior judge to his right, the next most senior to his left, and then alternating so that the most junior justice sits at the far end of the bench on the chief's left.

In the center chair sat William Hubbs Rehnquist, whom President Reagan had named the preceding spring as the sixteenth chief justice of the United States. Rehnquist had originally been appointed to the Court by Richard Nixon in 1971, and in his fifteen terms as an associate justice had earned a reputation as perhaps the best legal mind on the bench and certainly its most conservative. Although his opinions could be devastating in their logic, and his dissents especially sarcastic regarding the alleged mushiness of majority liberal opinions, Rehnquist got on well with his colleagues. The man had a sense of humor; he liked to laugh and had a reputation as a practical joker within the Court. He and Thurgood Marshall, another man who liked to laugh, once kept up a mock feud for weeks while their clerks grew increasingly anxious.

Woodside had no illusions that he might win over the chief justice. Ever since *Bakke*, Rehnquist had been a firm opponent of affirmative action and had voted against preferential hiring plans in every case the Court had decided. Rehnquist believed that if the country meant to put racial and gender discrimination behind it, then it should do so; preferential hiring plans merely substituted one form of bias for another. The chief justice had voted against gender discrimination and in fact had written the opinion holding that sexual harassment constituted a form of gender discrimination. But in this case, without a record of clear discrimination, Rehnquist would see the Santa Clara plan as another example of muddle-headed liberal social engineering.

To the chief's immediate right sat the most senior, and most liberal, member of the Court, William J. Brennan, Jr., whom Dwight Eisenhower had named to the bench in 1956. On almost any issue, Brennan could be expected to vote exactly opposite to Rehnquist, but like the chief, Brennan enjoyed good collegial relations, thanks to his warmth and buoyant optimism. Almost from the time he joined the Court, Brennan had been the political strategist of the liberal wing. During the fifties and sixties, he had been Earl Warren's closest adviser, and the two men would meet prior to the weekly conferences to plan strategy. The former chief justice, Warren Burger, had found Brennan a judicial pain through most of his tenure, as the senior justice had easily outmaneuvered Burger, cobbing together majorities on a variety of issues ranging from freedom of speech to rights of the accused.

Brennan strongly endorsed affirmative action and had written the Court's opinion in *Weber* and other cases. He also opposed gender discrimination in any form, and although he had been unable to convince a majority of his colleagues, he had tried to elevate gender to the same status as race in equal protection cases. There seemed no question that Brennan would support the Santa Clara plan.

To Rehnquist's left sat Byron R. White, former all-American athlete, Rhodes scholar, and professional football player. He had been a deputy attorney general in the Kennedy administration, and the president, a long-time friend, had named him to the Court in 1962. Some commentators labeled White as Kennedy's Warren, in that just as Dwight Eisenhower had been disappointed in the path Earl Warren took, so Kennedy would have been disappointed in White, who over the years had gravitated to the conservative side of the Court. This observation would be only partially true. Kennedy's liberalism had been relative; in some areas, such as civil rights, he had led the fight, but in others he had had little interest.

White's record on the Court showed him to be a strong defender of minority rights and an opponent of school segregation. But White had been tough-minded on issues such as rights of the accused and freedom of the press and in general could best be described as a rigorous pragmatist and a centrist, even if he tended to lean right of center. His record on affirmative action gave hope neither to Woodside nor Brooks; he had supported preferential plans but had usually demanded that they be narrowly tailored to remedy prior discrimination. How he voted in this case might well depend on the oral argument; White had a reputation as an exacting, relentless questioner.

Next to Brennan sat Thurgood Marshall, the Court's first and only black member. Marshall had been the chief architect of the NAACP's long and ultimately successful campaign to overturn racial segregation in the nation's schools and had himself argued *Brown* before the high court. Kennedy had named Marshall as a federal appeals judge, and then Lyndon Johnson had called him to Washington to be the solicitor general, the nation's lawyer, before nominating him to the Supreme Court in 1967.

On the bench, Marshall had remained a strong opponent of discrimination in any form, but he had never carved out his own jurisprudential niche. A liberal, he invariably voted the way Brennan did, leading some Court-watchers to claim that Brennan had two votes on any issue. Certainly in affirmative action, Marshall could be counted upon to support the county plan.

On the other side of the bench sat Harry A. Blackmun of Minnesota, named to the Court by Nixon in 1970. Blackmun had tended to vote with the conservatives in the early seventies, especially with his good friend, Chief Justice Warren Burger. By the end of the decade, however, Blackmun had traversed considerable jurisprudential ground and more often than not would be found voting along with Brennan and Marshall. Best known as the author of the 1973 abortion decision, *Roe v. Wade*, Blackmun had been a consistent defender of women's equality and had in general supported affirmative action. Both Woodside and Brooks assumed he would be a vote for the county.

Next in seniority came one of the most influential members of the Court, Lewis F. Powell, Jr., of Virginia. Appointed to the bench in 1972 after a distinguished career as a practicing attorney, Powell had emerged as the leader of the Court's centrist bloc. He could be tough on criminal procedure questions, but he had helped expand the reach of the First Amendment's Speech Clause and, like his fellow Virginians Thomas Jefferson and James Madison, believed in full separation of church and state.

His record on both affirmative action and women's issues made it clear that neither side could take his vote for granted. Powell had written the Court's opinion in *Bakke* that essentially said one could have race-conscious preferential plans, but only sometimes, depending on the circumstances; and circumstances usually, but not always, required a showing of prior discrimination. Powell had also followed a centrist path on women's issues; he had helped elevate scrutiny of gender discrimination claims to a so-called "intermediate" level but had been unwilling to accord gender the same constitutional status as race. Both sides knew that if they were to win, they would have to secure Lewis Powell's vote.

John Paul Stevens, appointed in 1975, had a reputation as the Court's ultimate independent, a man who eschewed legal dogmatism in favor of a case-by-case pragmatism. In many ways, Stevens reminded one of Potter Stewart, who in his tenure on the bench had also been very much a common law judge, one who looked at the results as well as the reasoning behind a case. Stevens's record on affirmative action had been mixed, as befitted a member of the centrist bloc. Brooks believed he would vote for the county, based on his dissent in the *Wygant* case; Woodside considered him a question mark.

At the far end of the bench on the chief's right sat Sandra Day O'Connor, the first woman appointed to the Court. Ronald Reagan had promised in his 1980 campaign to name a woman, but he wanted one who would be a conservative, tough on criminal procedure and opposed to social engineering schemes such as affirmative action. When he named O'Connor to the bench in 1981, he thought he had found just the right person. In her first few terms, O'Connor had tended to keep a low profile, and for the most part voted along with her former law school classmate, Bill Rehnquist.

But as she gained confidence on the bench, O'Connor started displaying a strong streak of independence, a development that came as no surprise to the people who had known her for years. By the 1986 term, while still voting with the conservatives on many issues, she had moved closer to the centrists, and in some cases began to play a Powell-like role, seeking an acceptable consensus between liberals and conservatives. As the only woman on the Court, she also proved particularly sensitive to so-called women's issues. Though not totally comfortable with *Roe*, she did not necessarily oppose the right of a woman to gain an abortion. And her own experience made her especially receptive to questions of gender discrimination.

After graduating second in her class at Stanford Law School, O'Connor had had difficulty in getting a job. One firm did offer to hire her, but as a legal secretary. None of these firms had ever hired a woman as a lawyer, she later recalled, and they were still not prepared to do so. Eventually she found jobs as a deputy county attorney and as a civilian lawyer for the army, but the experience remained with her; when questions of job discrimination came before the Court, Sandra O'Connor could identify with the plaintiff in ways that none of her white male colleagues could. Both Brooks and Woodside recognized the importance of O'Connor's vote; both had targeted her and Powell as key to their winning.

At the other end of the bench sat the Court's most junior member, Antonin Scalia, whom Reagan had just named to take Rehnquist's place as associate justice. Scalia, both as an appeals judge and as a law school professor, had shown himself to be literate, very bright, and very conservative. Scalia believed in a strict separation of powers and disdained extensive governmental remedies for social problems. Everyone knew where he stood on affirmative action — against it. In a caustic critique of affirmative action, he had once proposed the RJHS plan, the Restorative Justice Handicapping System, by which individuals would get points based on their ethnic and racial backgrounds to determine how much they owed society, or society owed them.

Brooks figured she could rely only on Rehnquist and Scalia, with White a wild card; Brennan, Marshall, Blackmun, and Stevens would vote for the affirmative action plan. In order to win, then, she needed to convince White, Powell, and O'Connor; the loss of even one would mean defeat. Woodside's head count looked similar to Brooks's. Rehnquist, Scalia, and White would vote for Paul Johnson; Brennan, Marshall, and Blackmun would support the county plan. Stevens might, after *Wygant*, stay with the liberals, but not definitely. Powell and O'Connor would be the swing votes; he had to win at least one of them.

Johnson was the second case the Court heard that morning, and at 11:03 A.M., Chief Justice Rehnquist turned to Constance Brooks, standing at the lectern, and nodded that she could proceed.

"Thank you, Mr. Chief Justice, and may it please the Court."

There is a great deal of debate over how much, if at all, the oral argument affects the decisions of the Court. William O. Douglas believed it made no difference and rarely participated in any questioning. He would answer his mail and write his opinions while listening with half an ear to the discussion. Oliver Wendell Holmes also used the time during oral argument to write letters, complaining that "one has to listen to discourses dragging slowly along after one has seen the point and made up one's mind."

Most justices, however, believe it does make a difference. Brennan had said that "often my idea of how a case shapes up is changed by oral argument." Chief Justice Rehnquist agreed and noted that in a "significant minority" of cases, oral argument swayed his opinion. Moreover, there is the symbolic value of oral argument in our democratic system. It is the only public part of the Supreme Court's work, the only time the people can see the nation's highest tribunal in operation.

In oral argument, what the justices do not want to hear is a repetition of the brief, and they do not want to have an attorney read to them. In fact, in 1980 the Court revised its rules to include this admonishment: "The Court looks with disfavor on any oral argument that is read from a prepared brief."

What the justices are seeking is illumination. If the briefs failed, in their opinion, to cover a point of law adequately, they may look to the oral argument to elucidate a point. They may also want to know what effect a particular decision will have. Court decisions are normally prospective, that is, they affect only future conditions and will not remedy current or past grievances. But if, for example, the Court rules that the state must provide lawyers at the first appeals stage, what impact will that have on crowded court calendars or on the administrative costs of the criminal justice system? They may also want to know how, in this particular situation, a change in the law will serve a useful purpose.

These questions may arise from the counsel's argument, but a justice can ask any question he or she wants at any time, and some justices have been known to press their questions with fierce determination. Felix Frankfurter in one case interrupted a lawyer ninety-three times during two hours of oral argument. In the midst of one exchange William O. Douglas intervened to help the hard-pressed attorney. An annoyed Frankfurter asked the lawyer, "I thought *you* were arguing this case?" "I am," came the reply, "but I can use all the help I can get." Such hectoring of counsel often annoys the other members of the bench, but it is one of the prerogatives of a justice to ask whatever he or she pleases, and very often the counsel's valuable time dwindles away in response to questions that may, or may not, further one's case.

As a strategy, therefore, one tries to get one's major points in as quickly as possible, and Connie Brooks did just that. She wanted the Court to apply the *Wygant* criteria so that a public employer could not have a preferential hiring program that did not address a specific record of discrimination. Moreover, such a plan had to be narrowly tailored and not unnecessarily trammel on the rights of innocent parties. Santa Clara County had never gone through the process of establishing a record of discrimination that needed remedial action, but the district court had heard evidence of a clear case of discrimination against Paul Johnson.

A minute-and-a-half went by, and then came the first question. "If a statistical imbalance in the work force is evident," Justice Stevens asked, "and they adopt an affirmative action plan, isn't it apparent on its face that it's remedial in the sense they're trying to remedy the imbalance?"

Brooks had anticipated this question, and had an answer — imbalances are not always the result of discrimination.

"So you say just statistical imbalance will never justify by itself an affirmative action?"

"I don't believe that it should," she responded, "and let me explain why." She started to say something about good intentions are not enough under Title VII criteria, when Justice White interrupted.

"What about *Weber?* [Do] you think in *Weber* the plan adopted was to remedy past discrimination?"

Yes, she agreed, but similar evidence of discrimination did not exist here; the county had only a single statistic — no women in the skilled-craft category — and that by itself should have no bearing on promotion decisions.

Justice O'Connor wanted to hear more about this and began pressing Brooks on the level of evidence she believed necessary to establish a case for discrimination. After all, here one had a category of 278 skilled positions and not one woman in any of them. "And you think this is not enough for the employer to think that there might be a firm basis here?"

Not in this case, Brooks replied, because the record established that social and attitudinal reasons, not discrimination, caused the statistical imbalance.

Justice Stevens joined O'Connor in pressing Brooks for the criteria that should be applied, and whether the agency's work force could legitimately be compared to the area labor pool, in which qualified women certainly existed.

Yes, Brooks agreed, the relevant labor market had to be one consideration, but statistics by themselves could not justify a preferential hiring plan. There had to be clear evidence that discrimination existed, and equally clear guidelines on how a public employer could go about remedying actual discrimination. The justices did not interrupt, so Brooks pressed on, reiterating the points she wanted the Court to remember. The plan had not been narrowly tailored; the aims had been too vague; the plan had no limits, only indefinite goals that too easily coerced particular divisions to make them into attainable quotas; it had no protection for innocent white males like Paul Johnson.

The Court, however, could not seem to shake itself of the statistical imbalance. Let's suppose, Stevens said, that the plan identified a substantial work pool, such as 238 skilled-craft positions, in which there were absolutely no women, and said that as an objective, the agency should hire the first qualified woman who applies for the job, just to break the pattern and get some representation. Would that be invalid?

Brooks cleverly rephrased the question to make it less abstract and said that it would be invalid, because in the instant case, the county already had women actively in the work force who would be in line for promotion.

"You're saying promotions always have to be made on merit, then?"

"I think that once you've opened the doors and provided for equal opportunity, it's appropriate to have these employees moving up through the work force based on the merit system."

"I agree it's appropriate. Do you think the statute requires that all promotions be made on merit . . . in the absence of any proof of past discrimination?"

"Convincing evidence, yes, Your Honor."

Justice White wanted to know whether Brooks thought that the *Weber* decision required proof of past discrimination, and she said it did, but in Santa Clara there had been no proof. Moreover, the plan would have been defective even if there had been evidence because it failed to meet the other *Weber* criteria. Justice Blackmun at this point wanted to know why the Court should not make this just a straightforward application of *Weber.*

That case had dealt with hiring, Brooks explained, which diffused the burden of the remedy, whereas the Santa Clara plan denied Paul Johnson a promotion he had already earned; he, and only he, bore the burden of the plan.

Justice Scalia had been pondering the evidentiary question and the fact that the Court had previously recognized that an employer did not have to admit past discrimination openly in order to establish a remedial plan. Brooks seemed to be saying that there had to be a clear record of past bias; the employer would have to admit that it had discriminated, and thus open itself to endless lawsuits. How would Brooks get an employer out of this dilemma — of having to admit to discrimination in order to justify the affirmative action plan, and thus be vulnerable to suit, or denying any bias, avoiding lawsuits, but leaving the discriminatory procedures in place?

It was a good question, one that had bedeviled the county and other employers considering preferential plans. Brooks did not have a clear answer — the employer only needs to show "some" evidence, "some" proof that he at least went through a process to examine the situation. "The employer is not necessarily required to prove to a certainty that he's discriminated."

You mean, Scalia continued, that all he has to show is he *may* have been discriminating?

"Exactly."

"But no employer's going to like to do that. I mean, you're just developing evidence for somebody else to use in a later suit against you."

Perhaps, Brooks replied, but Title VII says you cannot discriminate against your employees. A preferential plan discriminates, and so to justify it you have to prove there's a problem that needs remediation of this form. Brooks tried to show what would constitute minimal evidence that would not get an employer in trouble. Statistics would be the starting point, but they needed more than just evidence of a statistical imbalance.

Justice White had been listening to this exchange, and it troubled him. Suppose you have a Title VII case, he asked. "The plaintiff gets through with his case or her case and the only proof is racial imbalance, and there's a motion to dismiss."

That motion should be denied, Brooks said, "because statistical imbalances, if there's no explanation, do establish a case."

"Well," White pressed, "if that makes out a prima facie case in a Title VII case, just racial imbalance, what's the employer to do then — how can he win the case? Proving there isn't racial imbalance or proving that, what, there is no racial discrimination?"

"The employer can come forward with a number of explanations . . . to explain the statistical imbalance by reasons other than discrimination."

The response did not satisfy White, who wanted a real nuts-and-bolts answer. Look, he said, an employer has a racially imbalanced work force, and he goes to his attorney. If there is a suit under Title VII, the very fact of the imbalance means that the suit will survive a motion to dismiss. What the employer wants to know is, "Should I do something about it?" And if the employer does nothing, what will that mean in a Title VII suit?

"And that's exactly why having the employer consider statistical imbalances and look for explanations and then take a remedy before he gets sued would solve the problem."

Connie Brooks looked at her watch; she had used up twenty-five minutes, and, as the petitioner, had the right to save some time for rebuttal. She informed the Court that she wanted to reserve the rest of her time, but Justice White had not finished. "Did you just give away your case or not?" he asked. After all, Santa Clara County had evidently done just what Brooks had said it should do — considered the statistical imbalance, looked for an explanation, and then imposed a remedy to head off lawsuits.

No, we did not give away our case, she responded, because the county never went through the process, they never tried to find out why the statistical imbalance existed. If they had, the facts would have showed them that the cause was attitudinal and not a result of discrimination.

Rehnquist, recognizing that Brooks wanted to keep some time, brought the exchange to a close. He turned to the respondent's table. "We'll hear now from you, Mr. Woodside."

A benefit of being respondent's counsel is that one can listen to the Court's questions, pick out what issues seem to concern the justices most, and then play to those issues. Woodside had prepared some points to start with, but when he heard White ask Brooks what the employer should do, and what the employer's attorney should advise, he decided to take advantage of that opening. He also knew that by picking up on the question, he was taking a gamble, since White had a reputation of engaging counsel in long discussions that would not leave enough time to make all the necessary points. Hiding his nervousness under a patina of calm, Steven Woodside walked to the lectern.

"May it please the Court, I'd like to begin by answering the questions that Justice White just posed. With no women out of 238 skilled-craft workers . . . I think there would be a prima facie case."

White immediately picked up the point and wanted to know if a suit would survive a motion for dismissal on the basis of the statistical disparity alone.

"Absolutely, Your Honor."

"But it would not mean that the employer would necessarily lose the case?"

No, Woodside responded, not necessarily. "We would have the burden of articulating nondiscriminatory reasons for this particular imbalance. And I think on the facts of this case which are in the record, we would not have been able to meet that burden."

Six years after the initial complaint, four years after Judge Ingram heard the original suit, Santa Clara County finally came as close as it would to admitting that there had been discrimination against women.

The pragmatic White pondered Woodside's answer for a moment and then returned to the practical consequences of what he had said. In other words, the Justice said, if there is a statistical imbalance, then the employer must consider whether to take remedial steps.

That would be right, Woodside agreed.

But shouldn't the employer go on and say, "Well, I think I can still win because I have a neutral explanation."

"As I tried to make clear with the facts of this case —"

"Forget these facts," White interrupted. "Do you think the employer need not go on and say that I do or I don't have a neutral explanation?"

Yes, Woodside said, the employer should act immediately on the imbalance alone, because, as Justice Scalia had said earlier, to fail to act puts the employer between the rock and the hard place.

White seemed dissatisfied with the answer and pressed on for a few more questions until the chief justice asked if this did not constitute a disagreement over whether the burden of proof should be on the plaintiff or on the defendant. Woodside agreed, but before he could explain, Justice Powell caught his attention.

According to the record, the district court had found that there never had been any discrimination against women by the Transportation Agency. In fact, none was occurring at the time of the trial.

Woodside saw "danger" written all over this question and tried to evade it.

"That, Your Honor, was not a litigated issue in the case."

Powell would not be put off. "It did make that finding?"

Yes, Woodside conceded, it had.

"Did the court of appeals hold it clearly erroneous?"

No, it had not, but the question should not be whether the agency had discriminated. "The relevant inquiry," Woodside explained using language taken from earlier decisions by Powell and O'Connor, "should be whether or not the employer believed and had a firm basis to conclude that it may have discriminated against women, based on its own knowledge of the statistics."

Justice O'Connor, the other critical swing vote, wanted Woodside to explain a bit more about the affirmative action plan, about how the goals had been determined. Did the county go to the percentage of women in the local labor market or just to the number of women who had the requisite skills?

This, of course, had been one of the weak points of the county plan in that it had never clearly articulated these standards. Woodside explained that the plan had a mix of both plans.

"So," O'Connor interjected, "you concede that this employer affirmative action plan was not geared to the number of qualified women in the pool of labor?"

"No, Your Honor, I don't concede that," he responded quickly, recognizing that if the Court believed there had been no rational relationship between the plan and the local work force demography, it would find against the county. There was a relationship, a goal set of three women out of fifty-five expected new skilled hires in 1983, and that reflected the available work force.

O'Connor wanted to know where she could find that.

In the joint appendix, he said. A few seconds later, a page handed O'Connor the appendix, and she spent much of the rest of the hour looking through it, while listening to the argument.

Justice Scalia had pushed Connie Brooks on the dilemma of an employer faced with a statistical imbalance and subject to suit, and now he put Woodside through his paces.

Long-term goals are very nice, but how do they relate to this case? "We're not trying somebody else who came up after there was a three-out-of-fifty-five requirement. . . . This is Mr. Johnson's case, I thought, and he's complaining about being denied a promotion." The plan had a long-term requirement of 36.4 percent of women in the skilled crafts. Didn't that deny Johnson his promotion?

No, Woodside explained, it did not. The plan did not set a quota, it set long-term goals and merely said that when making promotion decisions, the director of the agency should give consideration to the existence of an imbalance. Woodside took the opportunity to deny an assertion that Connie Brooks had made earlier, that in such a situation a woman would always be hired over a man. "There is no evidence," Woodside explained, "to indicate that in every case women would get the promotion. Indeed, the facts are to the contrary."

Scalia then returned to the issue O'Connor had raised earlier, whether the plan related to the number of women in the local labor pool or just to the percentage of skilled women. "Is it your position that the county as an employer can set an affirmative action plan goal that is geared to the number of women in the labor force in the county generally, as opposed to the number of qualified women in the available pool?"

"Yes, Your Honor," he replied, because "one would ordinarily expect in jobs throughout an agency that [women] would be comprised, absent discrimination, of roughly their numbers that exist in the general labor pool."

A seemingly astounded Scalia leaned forward to make sure he had heard right. Do you mean, he asked, that "it is statistically reasonable to expect as many women to be working on road crews and to believe that if there aren't that proportion there must be discrimination?"

Yes, Woodside agreed, there would be an inference of discrimination.

"What is that based on? Human experience or some governmental policy?"

"I think it is based on both human experience and governmental policy."

"On human experience?"

"Yes, Your Honor. I think women do seek these jobs — "

"In this country?"

"Yes."

At this exchange, Diane Joyce had to struggle to keep from bursting out laughing. She thought Scalia was joking, that he was just trying to help Woodside along by pointing out the absurdity of the situation. Later, when Kristy Sermersheim and Suzanne Wilson explained that Scalia had not been kidding, that he did not believe that women wanted to work on road crews, Diane began worrying that the case would be lost.

Before Scalia could push this much further, Justice Stevens began asking a series of questions that Woodside interpreted as trying to be helpful. Tell us, Stevens said, how you think your plan accords with previous cases decided by the Court, and how you can justify giving relief to a nonvictim.

If an employer had a firm basis to believe that its practices had been discriminatory, "then the employer could voluntarily take affirmative action which is not victim-specific."

"Do you think our cases said that the circumstances must evidence particularly egregious instances of discrimination?"

No, Woodside said, they didn't have to be particularly egregious. If a prima facie case can be made out, then the employer can act.

There was no finding of egregious discrimination in this case, was there?

No, Woodside agreed, but he reminded the Court that in addition to the statistical imbalance, the trial had produced evidence of the agency's own practices that had been overtly discriminatory.

Stevens now tried to sum up Woodside's argument, to be sure that he understood it correctly.

"You're asserting that a government always has the right to institute a plan that permits discrimination in hiring and in promotion on the basis of race or sex whenever its work force does not contain the same proportion of race, minority race, or that sex, as the work force at large . . . that statistical disparity is enough to justify an affirmative action plan, that is to say discrimination by the government on the basis of race?"

Woodside did not like the way Stevens had phrased it and started to hedge on how large a statistical disparity would be required and whether there were any other explanations, when Scalia interrupted.

"Well, now you sound like the other side. Now you're saying that it isn't enough to just have a statistical disparity, that the employer has to have some reason to believe that the statistical disparity is the result of discrimination."

No, that's not what he meant, Woodside said. The statistical disparity is the starting point. When you have additional facts, as you do in this case, then you know you have a discrimination problem and have to act. Moreover, in response to another question by Stevens, Woodside insisted that Diane Joyce did not get the job just because she was a woman. It had not been automatic; she had met the qualifications, and under the plan her gender had been an important, but not the only, consideration. Women did not get an automatic preference under the plan.

This response prompted Scalia again, who pressed Woodside that Johnson had had his eye on the job, had taken a demotion to obtain better qualifications, and had scored higher than Joyce in the tests. "He was selected and would have gotten the job but for the fact of the affirmative action program. . . . Isn't that the facts of the case?"

Had Scalia asked this earlier, before Woodside had overcome his initial nervousness, the blunt hostility might have thrown him. But so far he had been able to hold his own on the questioning, and he knew that he could not let Scalia characterize the case this way. He reminded the Court that Joyce had also competed for the job, that she also had worked on the road crews, that she had achieved a qualifying score. Given this situation, as well as the statistical imbalance, the Court should allow local authorities to make decisions, based on local circumstances and the employer's knowledge of the facts, that would be best and as fair as possible to all concerned.

The last few minutes of respondent's time turned into a colloquy among Woodside, Stevens, and Scalia about what an employer had to take into account to be fair to the work force, to minorities, and to avoid the rock-and-hard-place situation. Stevens put forward a hypothetical situation in which there are no women in the work force of 238 people. The employer knows that but also knows that no woman has ever applied, so he has never discriminated. He knows he has never discriminated. Would he be able to adopt an affirmative action program?

No, Woodside replied, "I don't think he could — "

Before he could finish the sentence, Scalia jumped in. "Even though that would make out a prima facie case of employment discrimination?"

"That's the difficulty," Woodside said. "Given Justice Stevens's hypothetical, there is no prima facie case because — "

No, Scalia said, given what you told us before, all the employer has to do is show an imbalance.

But Justice Stevens, Woodside continued, is suggesting that there is a legitimate explanation for the imbalance.

Would that be a defense to the prima facie case?

Yes, Woodside agreed.

Scalia pounced. "He has a prima facie case, and I thought you had been saying that so long as there is a prima facie case he can institute an affirmative action plan."

Well, yes, Woodside admitted, and I tried to —

"So maybe," Scalia said with a big grin, "you should have given a different answer to Justice Stevens."

"I'm sorry," Woodside said, but Scalia's grin was infectious, and although there is supposed to be little or no levity in the nation's highest court, laughter swept across the courtroom, a welcome break from the tension for the audience, the attorneys, and above all the justices.

A smiling Stevens ventured, "I should have asked Justice Scalia," and the audience continued to chuckle.

Woodside saw the amber warning signal on the lectern and decided to take advantage of the situation.

"I have nothing further to add. Thank you."

———

The chief justice informed Constance Brooks that she had four minutes left of her time for rebuttal.

Brooks wanted to use those minutes to press home her main points, especially that an employer needs more than a prima facie case to institute an affirmative action plan, that it had to explore the reasons for the statistical discrepancies.

Before she had gone very far on this, Justice O'Connor, who had been trying to figure out the proportional goals from the joint appendix, decided to press Brooks on this issue.

"What difference does it make whether the proper proportion in this particular labor pool, if we're playing statistics, was 30 percent or 5 percent? What difference does it make, inasmuch as there were no women in this job category at the time anyway?" Because, Brooks replied, unless the numbers bear some relationship to the relevant pool, in this case the number of women qualified for the job, then the plan is arbitrary and trammels the interests of innocent people like Paul Johnson. You cannot just allow the employer to slip in whatever figures it wants.

What if the employer had used the right percentages, would that have made this an acceptable plan?

No, it would not, and without any further interruptions, Brooks reiterated the points she had made earlier about the defects in the plan. There were women in the work force and in nontraditional jobs, so the county had not discriminated; it had not investigated the situation to determine whether there had been discrimination. She wanted to remind the Court of another consideration.

"I think there's another factor here," she began, when the amber light on the lectern switched to red, the signal that her time had expired. It is the responsibility of the chief justice to make sure that counsel do not exceed their allotted time. It was said that when Charles Evans Hughes sat in the center chair, he would interrupt an attorney in the middle of the word "if" when the red light flashed. The gentler Rehnquist would never snap that quickly, but neither would he allow her to continue.

"Your time has expired, Ms. Brooks."

Connie Brooks thanked the Court and sat down, and at three minutes past noon, the chief justice announced that the case was submitted.

———

After the Court recessed for lunch, the Santa Clara crew went down the street and crowded around a table in an Italian restaurant — Steve Woodside, Ann Ravel, Suzanne Wilson, Zoe Lofgren, Kristy Sermersheim, Diane and Donna Joyce. They congratulated Woodside and then began analyzing the case. Suzanne Wilson thought that Scalia had behaved rudely in hectoring Steve, but a very relieved assistant county counsel said no, that had not been rudeness; it showed that the justices were really interested in the case. He felt certain they had grasped what he had to say. Suzanne Wilson, unfamiliar with the customs of oral argument, silently prayed that he was right.

"It was a scary, heady experience," she later recalled, "to have your affirmative action plan held in the hands of nine people who don't know your county, who don't know who we are and what we're about, and how the people in this county like this and keep electing the people who do these kind of things."

All they could do now, however, was wait.

CHAPTER 9

The Court Decides

The actual decision of a case takes place within a few days after oral argument, at the Court's next conference. Cases argued on Monday are discussed at the Wednesday afternoon conference; those argued on Tuesday and Wednesday are decided at the Friday morning session. A buzzer sounds in each justice's chambers five minutes before the meeting is scheduled to begin, calling them to the large conference room next to the chief justice's chambers, where after shaking hands with each other, they take their seats. The chief justice sits at one end of the large rectangular table, and the senior associate justice, William Brennan, sits at the other. On one side are the next three most senior members, White, Marshall, and Blackmun; across from them the four junior members, Powell, Stevens, O'Connor, and Scalia. Each justice will have some papers relating to the cases under discussion, such as notes taken during the oral argument or memorandums prepared by one of the clerks. A full set of briefs is available on a cart near the table. No law clerks, no secretaries, no one but the justices themselves take part in the conference; if there is a message for one of the justices, a member of the Marshal's Office will knock on the door, and the most junior member of the Court goes to get it and then hands it to whichever justice it is addressed.

The chief justice sets the agenda. Cases already heard at oral argument automatically are on the table, as well as petitions for certiorari and other business ready for decision. An individual justice may, as a matter of personal privilege, ask that an item be put off until the next meeting, but because of the Court's heavy workload, its members try to stick to the regular schedule as closely as possible.

The chief justice will introduce each case by briefly reviewing the facts and the lower court decision, and then indicate his understanding of the applicable law and how he intends to vote. The discussion then moves down the line of seniority, with each justice stating his or her view and vote; if someone is not sure, and wants to hear the other opinions first, he or she may abstain, and vote at the end. There is no separate ballot; each justice votes by indicating his or her stance.

The length of discussion, the acrimony or lack of it, depends on many circumstances aside from the actual issues in the case. Charles Evans Hughes ran a tight ship, and his ability succinctly to state the issues in a case meant that the ensuing discussion rarely involved more than an indication of the vote. His successor, Harlan Fiske Stone, wanted to encourage more give-and-take and soon lost control of the conference; debate over cases could drag on for hours, especially when Felix Frankfurter felt moved to lecture the brethren. Despite the controversial nature of many of the cases during his tenure, Earl Warren's political skills kept conferences on an even and peaceful keel. Warren Burger's personal kindness and warmth made him well-liked by the brethren outside the conference; inside, he managed to alienate several of the justices by his clumsy attempts to control votes and writing assignments.

After the discussion and vote, if the chief justice is in the majority, he assigns responsibility for the Court's opinion and keeps a tally of the assignments to ensure the workload is equitably distributed. In very important cases, the chief will usually take the opinion himself, to emphasize the Court's decision. On those occasions when the chief justice is in the minority, the senior justice in the majority assigns the opinion.

From all indications, most justices enter the conference knowing how they will vote. The ensuing discussion rarely wins converts, although in some very close cases a justice torn two ways may not actually decide which way to vote until he or she has heard the discussion. But if the conference is not critical to the vote, it is crucial in determining the substance of the Court's opinion. Five or more justices may agree in a particular case that the lower court decision should be overturned; they may not agree on the grounds for reversal. The conference discussion will indicate to whoever writes the opinion the jurisprudential parameters in which he or she must operate. Stay within those lines, and keep the majority; stray beyond them, and risk losing the majority on either the decision, its grounds, or both.

The *form* of the conference is well-known, but the actual *contents* are not. This is where the justices decide cases, and in 200 years they have remained very closemouthed about what transpires in the conference room. We can piece together some stories because in recent years the papers of some justices have become available to scholars, and William O. Douglas, for example, kept careful notes of conference discussions. In *Johnson* we get a fairly clear picture of each justice's views and how those views shaped the different opinions that the Court handed down.

Docket No. 85-1129, *Johnson v. Transportation Agency*, had been argued on a Wednesday morning, and the justices discussed it at their Friday morning conference on November 14, 1986. Chief Justice Rehnquist began the discussion with a brief precis of the facts. There had been a promotional opportunity; Diane Joyce had scored lower than Paul Johnson in the screening process; the district court had found the county's action in violation of Title VII; the court of appeals had reversed on the basis of *Weber*. Rehnquist found the county's plan flawed because it did not seem to have any end date; it would just always be there. Moreover, unlike *Weber*, which involved hiring and thus spread the burden, in this case Johnson had been rejected for a promotion, on the grounds of gender alone, and thus had to bear the entire burden by himself. No question existed that the county had instituted a gender-conscious plan, and the Court's previous cases held that before a public employer could adopt a race-conscious, or in this instance a gender-conscious plan, it had to make a prima facie case that the minority had actually been discriminated against. Although statistics will sometimes be sufficient to make the prima facie case, there are occasions when more evidence is necessary. He believed the record in this case, by itself, did not establish the prima facie case, although the statistic of no women in 238 positions certainly hinted at it. The chief justice believed that the solicitor general's proposal made sense, and he recommended sending the case back for reconsideration, to see whether there had been sufficient discrimination to warrant the plan.

When Rehnquist finished, William Brennan took the floor, and as the most consistent champion of affirmative action on the bench, it came as no surprise that he supported affirming the court of appeals.

Brennan had had a memo prepared by one of his clerks indicating the main points of law that he believed governed the case. Although Connie Brooks had wanted the Court to take *Wygant* as its standard, Brennan insisted that the county's plan accorded with the Title VII criteria set out in *Weber*. The Court, he argued, should not decide this case on an equal protection analysis because that claim had neither been raised nor argued in the courts below; it had started as a Title VII case and should be decided as such.

Under the *Weber* criteria, employers did not have to admit past discrimination but show only "imbalances in traditionally segregated job categories." The county had demonstrated such an imbalance, and in several previous cases the Court had held that statistical disparities by themselves establish a prima facie case. If that were not enough, testimony at the trial confirmed the existence of past employment practices that disadvantaged women.

What about Paul Johnson? Did the plan unnecessarily trammel his rights, contrary to *Weber*'s imperative? Brennan did not believe it did. No specific positions had been set aside for women; rather, gender became just one more factor to consider on a case-by-case basis. It is true that Johnson had not received the job, but he had not lost anything he already had, such as seniority and salary. In a growing department, it would be reasonable to expect there would be other promotional opportunities for him.

Brennan disagreed with the chief justice over the duration of the county plan. It would not operate indefinitely, he insisted, but would be reviewed annually and continuously adjusted to measure progress toward its goal. Summing up, Brennan believed that Santa Clara's plan "was adopted on the basis of even more striking evidence than put forth in *Weber*, and has a far less intrusive impact on non-protected employees than the plan upheld in that case."

For Justice White, who spoke next, the significant fact seemed to be that the case involved a public rather than a private employer; this made it more like *Wygant* than *Weber* and imposed a higher standard of review. A public employer had to show some evidence of egregious discrimination, and he did not believe that Diane Joyce had ever faced that experience. In order to establish a plan, White believed, the standard of proof should be that the employer would lose a Title VII

{ *Affirmative Action on Trial* }

case, and he found very little evidence in the record to meet that standard.

The chief justice looked next at Thurgood Marshall, who grumbled "affirm." Harry Blackmun, sitting beside Marshall, agreed with Brennan that the Court should not take up Brooks's invitation to apply an equal protection claim. Moreover, it really did not matter whether one started out under the Equal Protection Clause or the Civil Rights Act; one still had to demonstrate that discrimination had existed, and statistical evidence of a racial or gender imbalance established the prima facie case. Under Title VII, he thought the record straightforward enough to justify the plan, and he voted to affirm.

Across the table, Lewis Powell looked up from his notes and agreed that the case had to be decided on Title VII, not on constitutional grounds. There had not been purposeful discrimination, but the record certainly showed a numerical imbalance. Powell believed the county plan resembled thousands across the country, and though the numbers could have been more reflective of the available work force, he believed the plan set goals, not quotas. He would vote to affirm.

John Paul Stevens agreed with Powell that the record did not show purposeful discrimination. Stevens, who had not participated in the *Weber* case, had on more than one occasion indicated that he believed it had been wrongly decided. But, he said, *Weber* was the law for Title VII cases and therefore controlled here; he agreed that the county plan met its criteria.

At the oral argument, Sandra Day O'Connor had given every indication that she thought the plan defective because the numbers did not match the percentage of qualified women in the work force, but she did not pursue this idea at the conference. The employer had decided it was wrong to have no qualified women in one of the skilled-job categories, and under perfectly proper personnel procedures, it had chosen Diane Joyce for the job. O'Connor disagreed with White that Joyce had not faced discrimination; this woman had filed grievances before and could well have scared the employer with an implicit threat to sue.

Even before O'Connor spoke, it had become clear that a majority supported affirming the court of appeals and upholding the county plan. But the Court's junior justice, Antonin Scalia, wanted to tell his colleagues that he thought this was a terrible plan and that it would be awful to make employers institute preferential plans on the basis of numbers alone.

Connie Brooks and Steve Woodside had thought it would be very close, probably 5 to 4; in fact, six of the justices — Brennan, Marshall, Blackmun, Powell, Stevens, and O'Connor — voted to endorse the plan; Rehnquist, White, and Scalia wanted to overturn it. Both key center votes, Powell and O'Connor, the two that Brooks and Woodside recognized as crucial, had come down in favor of affirmative action.

With the chief justice in the minority, the senior justice, William Brennan, would determine who wrote the opinion for the Court. Later that afternoon he dropped a note to Rehnquist that he would try his hand at the two affirmative action suits decided that morning, *Johnson* and *Paradise*, the Alabama state trooper case.

———

Ultimately each justice is responsible for opinions in his or her name, but nearly all of them rely on clerks to write at least a first draft. The normal practice is for justices, immediately following conference, to meet with their clerks to go over the cases. They then assign the cases to specific clerks, with instructions on the approach the justice wants to take.

Until World War II, most justices had only one clerk. Following the war, the number of clerks began to increase, so that by the October 1986 term, each chamber had four clerks. On the positive side of this proliferation, each member of the Court could handle more paperwork, go through the ever-increasing number of cert and pauper petitions, and have better staff work in preparation for oral argument and conference. On the downside, it has led to a geometric expansion of opinions, as well as the size of opinions. As late as the 1940s and early 1950s, justices in general agreement with a draft of the majority opinion would swallow their qualms about particular sections. Now, with three or four clerks for assistance, it is no trouble at all to have one of them draft a concurrence or a dissent focusing on a limited question of fact or law.

In William Brennan's chambers, the justice left a fair amount of

　　　　{ *Affirmative Action on Trial* }

organizational responsibility to his staff. The four clerks divided up incoming cases and then did the necessary work on them, such as preparing bench memorandums prior to the oral argument or conference. *Johnson* wound up on the desk of Mitt Regan, Jr., a native of Houston who had originally gone into urban planning and had worked for the city of Alexandria as a planner before deciding on law school. He had done well at the Georgetown Law Center in Washington and then had clerked a year for Judge Ruth Bader Ginsberg in the D.C. Circuit, a place from which Brennan drew many of his clerks.

Shortly after Brennan returned from the conference, he sat down with Regan to go over his notes, indicating how the justices in favor of affirming the lower court differed in their views. Regan already knew much of this, since a prime form of communication, and often of negotiation in the Court, takes place among the clerks, who put forth their justice's view and in turn learn the special concerns of other chambers. Regan set about drafting an opinion for Brennan, and throughout the weeks and months that followed, he paid special attention to what the clerks in Lewis Powell's office said to him. Within two weeks, Regan had a draft in Brennan's hands, and after a minor editing, Brennan circulated the eighteen-page first iteration to his colleagues for their inspection.

Court opinions for the most part follow a set pattern. The first paragraph summarizes the specific question, notes the lower court decisions, and indicates whether the Court affirms, reverses, or remands. Next comes a fairly detailed statement of the facts, with copious references to the record. Finally, the opinion deals with the one or more issues of law that the justices have decided.

After relating the story of Joyce's promotion under the affirmative action plan and Johnson's suit, Brennan first dealt with whether Johnson had carried his burden of proving the plan invalid. In *Wygant* the previous term, the Court had held that an employer's plan would have the benefit of assumed validity by the courts; those claiming discrimination under the plan would have to prove that it had either violated equal protection claims or the criteria established in *Weber*. If a plaintiff could prove that race or gender had been taken into account in an employment decision, then the employer had to provide a nondiscriminatory rationale, and the existence of an affirmative action plan provided such a rationale. Contrary to what Connie Brooks had argued, Brennan held that an employer did not have to justify the plan; those attacking it had to prove it invalid. In this case, the gender imbalances provided a sufficient rationale for the county to establish an affirmative action plan, and no evidence produced by Johnson showed the plan as defective under *Weber*.

How would one assess the legality of the county's plan? *Weber* provided the criteria—it had to address the problem of racial (or gender) segregation and hierarchy, it could not unnecessarily trammel the interests of white (or male) employees, and it had to be narrowly tailored and of limited duration. Moreover, in his concurrence in *Weber*, Justice Blackmun had made clear that the decision did not require an employer to admit to prior discriminatory practices but need only point to a "conspicuous . . . imbalance in traditionally segregated job categories." The record here supported that claim by the county that it had addressed the problem, that it had not unnecessarily trammeled white male interests, and that the plan had a limited duration with narrowly drawn goals. The justification for instituting the plan lay in the numbers—no females in the 238 skilled-craft positions. Brennan then spent several pages showing how the Transportation Agency plan met the *Weber* criteria, concluding:

> Substantial evidence shows that the Agency has sought to take a moderate, gradual approach to eliminating the imbalance in its work force, one which establishes realistic guidance for employment decisions, and which visits minimal intrusion on the legitimate expectations of other employees. . . .

> We therefore hold that the Agency appropriately took into account as one factor the sex of Diane Joyce in determining that she should be promoted to the road dispatcher position. The decision to do so was made pursuant to an affirmative action plan that represents a moderate, flexible, case-by-case approach to effecting a gradual improvement in the representation of minorities and women in the Agency's work force. Such a plan is fully consistent with Title VII, for it embodies the contribution that voluntary employer action can make in eliminating the vestiges of discrimination in the workplace. Accordingly, the judgment of the Court of Appeals is *Affirmed*.

Although the opinion would go through five iterations, in substance the holding and rationale remained consistent throughout. Brennan distributed this first draft on the morning of December 1. That afternoon he had his first two responses. Thurgood Marshall wrote, "Dear Bill: Please join me," indicating he fully subscribed to the opinion.

Byron White had voted on the other side in conference, but because he had in the past supported some affirmative action plans, Brennan hoped that by emphasizing that the Santa Clara proposal met the *Weber* criteria, he might win White over. But White had been unconvinced and told Brennan that he would wait to see what the dissent might say.

The next day, John Paul Stevens signed on, but Antonin Scalia informed Brennan that he would be preparing a dissent, no great surprise following Scalia's comments in conference. And Brennan might also have anticipated the two-page memo he received from Sandra Day O'Connor. Though in agreement with "substantial portions" of the opinion and with the judgment, she found it troubling that the draft did not address the question of what precise evidence would be necessary to justify an affirmative action plan, the same issue that had concerned her during oral argument.

Brennan had interpreted *Weber* to mean that an employer had to show only a "manifest . . . imbalance in traditionally segregated job categories." She agreed that *Weber* could be read that way, but she believed more should be required, some "firm basis for believing that remedial action is required." Citing the ten-year-old decision in *Hazelwood School District v. United States* (1977), she suggested that a prima facie case under Title VII needed at the least some comparison of the women in the work force with those in the local demographic area having the relevant qualifications. She believed this did not contradict *Weber*, since that case dealt with *unskilled* workers, whereas *Hazelwood* and *Johnson* involved skilled categories.

O'Connor indicated that Brennan's opinion already headed in this direction in his discussion of statistics as a justification for a preferential hiring plan, and she believed that in this case the Transportation Agency had a firm basis, according to her criteria, for establishing the plan. But she wanted this spelled out more specifically and promised to circulate a partial concurrence as promptly as possible.

The entire tone of O'Connor's letter was friendly, and there was no question of her changing votes on the result. No judge, however, wants to write an opinion for the Court in which he or she cannot even get a majority to go along. O'Connor wanted a higher level of proof than Brennan, and her letter implied that if Brennan would adopt her standard, she would be glad to go along fully.

On Wednesday, December 3, Harry Blackmun joined the opinion. Brennan now had four votes, including his own, in full support of his draft, and O'Connor concurring in all but one section. One more join, and he would have to do only some stylistic editing. That Friday, however, Lewis Powell informed him that he shared O'Connor's concern that the adoption and implementation of a voluntary affirmative action plan should be based on a "reasonable comparison" of the percentages of the protected group in the available labor pool and in the employer's work force. He suggested modifying a paragraph in Brennan's draft to make this explicit and also suggested adding a footnote to the effect that "where the issue is properly raised, public employers must justify the adoption and implementation of a voluntary affirmative action plan under the equal protection clause. See *Wygant.*"

"If you prefer not to make these changes I will of course understand," Powell concluded. "I will join your judgment in any event, and will say in whatever I write that I agree for the most part with your opinion."

Brennan had his majority, but barely. O'Connor and Powell had both raised the issue of numbers, but with differing emphasis. For O'Connor, numbers provided the evidence supporting affirmative action; numbers also indicated the fairness and relevancy of the plan, that a direct link existed between the problem and the solution. Powell, on the other hand, saw the numbers as one more piece of the puzzle, an important piece to be sure, but one viewed in the light of other historical and social factors. Brennan had no problem incorporating Powell's suggested changes, practically word for word, in the second draft of his opinion, which he circulated on December 9. That afternoon, Powell informed Brennan that he would join the opinion.

Although Justice Stevens had indicated he would join Brennan's opinion, on December 18 he circulated the first draft of a concurrence. He still signed on both to the reasoning and result in Brennan's draft, but the changes that Brennan had put in to meet Powell's suggestions seemed to Stevens to narrow the opinion more than necessary. He wanted to emphasize that "the opinion does not establish the permissible outer limits of voluntary programs undertaken by employers to benefit disadvantaged groups."

Stevens first reviewed the Court's decisions interpreting how race-conscious affirmative action plans fit into Title VII's seemingly absolute prohibition against any preferment by race or gender. Had the Court adhered to a strict interpretation of the statute, Paul Johnson would win this case. But in *Bakke* and in *Weber*, a majority "interpreted the anti-discriminatory strategy of the statute in a fundamentally different way," allowing race to be taken into account. The two cases "are now an important part of the fabric of our law, and so must be taken into account in order to provide stability."

The "logic" of Title VII, Stevens believed, required that the courts leave "breathing room" for employer initiatives designed to benefit minority groups. As such, employers ought not be required to justify their behavior in terms of past conduct. The question should not be whether a particular employer had or had not discriminated in the past, but whether an affirmative action plan would benefit it in the future. Quoting from a recent law review article, Stevens pointed out that a school board might institute a plan not because of past discrimination, but to improve the quality of education. Businesses might establish preferential programs to improve their services to black constituencies or to avert racial tension or to increase the diversity of their work forces. Stevens saw these steps as legitimate rationales, which he wanted to emphasize constituted as strong a reason for establishing affirmative action plans as the proof of past discrimination. Because Brennan's opinion did not foreclose these options, Stevens still joined it.

Brennan had been waiting to see whether Sandra Day O'Connor would join the majority and, like Stevens, write a concurrence that emphasized her special understanding of one point, or whether she would concur only in the result. When he returned from the New Year's break, Brennan found O'Connor's draft. Quickly skimming through it, he saw exactly what he had hoped for — she had signed on both to the result and the reasoning and had written on the particular point that troubled her, the need by a public (as opposed to private) employer to show evidence of an imbalance in the work force.

Relying on her concurring opinion in *Wygant*, O'Connor noted that the Court had agreed that evidence of past discrimination by the employer — not social discrimination in general — provided sufficient justification for a race- or gender-conscious hiring plan. But although the employer did not have to point to "contemporaneous findings of actual discrimination," there had to be a firm basis for concluding that remedial action was necessary and that this evidentiary test could be met by showings of a statistical imbalance.

This had been, at least for her, the primary holding in *Wygant*, and although Brennan did not say so explicitly, she concluded that his opinion followed those principles. The fact that no woman — "the inexorable zero" — occupied a skilled-craft position, although women constituted 5 percent of the local labor pool of skilled workers, provided the necessary evidence of a prima facie Title VII case. Moreover, she agreed that the rights of male workers had not been unnecessarily trammeled, and the plan also fit the *Weber* requirement of narrow tailoring. She would, therefore, join the Court's opinion.

Although both Stevens and O'Connor still joined in his opinion, their interpretations of the predicates for a preferential hiring plan seemed diametrically opposed. Stevens wanted to allow employers great latitude in their justification, but O'Connor did not. In fact, in her concurrence she had specifically attacked Stevens's view as contrary to the Court's earlier holdings. Brennan leaned somewhat toward Stevens's view and did not want to force employers to show previous or present discrimination in order to institute affirmative action plans.

So on January 8, 1987, he circulated the third draft of his opinion, in which he added a paragraph and a footnote directly responding to O'Connor:

A manifest imbalance need not be such that it would support a prima facie case against the employer, as suggested in JUSTICE O'CONNOR's concurrence, since we do not regard as identical the constraints of Title VII and the federal constitution on voluntarily adopted affirmative action plans. Application of the "prima facie" standard in Title VII cases would be inconsistent with *Weber's* focus on statistical imbalance, and could inappropriately create a significant disincentive for employers to adopt an affirmative action plan. . . . A corporation concerned with maximizing return on investment, for instance, is hardly likely to adopt a plan if in order to do so it must compile evidence that could be used to subject it to a colorable Title VII suit.

In an accompanying footnote, Brennan explained that if the Court had applied O'Connor's suggested test in *Weber* it would not have found evidence of past discrimination, because in terms of *skilled* workers, there would have been no statistical imbalance: the lack of skilled minority workers in the employer's work force reflected their absence in the available labor pool. But that condition had resulted from years of prior discrimination in which blacks had been excluded from training programs. *Weber*, according to Brennan, thus stood for a more flexible approach to evaluating justifications for preferential plans.

With these alterations, Brennan lost O'Connor from his majority. That same day, she wrote that his additions "compel me to change my concurrence to an opinion concurring in the judgment. Apparently, you interpret *Weber* in a way I would not." She promised to make the necessary changes as soon as possible so as not to delay announcement of the decision. The next day she circulated a third draft, concurring in the judgment, but not in the reasoning, of the majority.

She wished to emphasize that, in her view, the same evidentiary standards applied to a public employer under Title VII as under the Equal Protection Clause, and this did not include, as Stevens seemed to suggest in his concurrence, evidence only of a general social discrimination. She interpreted the Court's prior decisions, especially in *Weber* and *Wygant*, as requiring "a firm basis for believing that remedial action is required, and that a statistical imbalance sufficient for a Title VII prima facie case would satisfy this firm basis requirement." Unfortunately, she wrote,

the Court today gives little guidance for what statistical imbalance is sufficient to support an affirmative action plan. Although the Court denies that a statistical imbalance need be sufficient for a prima facie case, the Court fails to suggest an alternative standard.

Because both *Wygant* and *Weber* attempt to reconcile the same competing concerns, I see no justification for the adoption of different standards for affirmative action under Title VII and the Equal Protection Clause.

Brennan pondered what changes, if any, he should make either to answer O'Connor's charge or to try to win her back to the majority. Before he circulated another draft, however, he wanted to see what the dissent would say. Whatever the reason for the delay, weeks went by with no further action on the case. Then on February 24, Antonin Scalia circulated the first draft of his dissent to the Court.

———

If there is any single document that can be said to epitomize conservative opposition to affirmative action, it could well be Justice Scalia's dissent in this case. He began with an appeal to read the plain language of Title VII, language "with a clarity which, had it not proven so unavailing, one might well recommend as a model of statutory draftsmanship." He then quoted from the section that prohibited the use of race or sex for employment decisions and charged the majority with converting it into a guarantee that race or sex *will be used*, a process, he claimed, that had been going on for over a decade. "We effectively replace the goal of a discrimination-free society with the quite incompatible goal of proportionate representation by race and by sex in the workplace."

Scalia's well-written and well-organized opinion could leave no one in doubt of the intellectual power he would bring to bear on the conservative side of the bench. In his three-part opinion he first described the plan and its effect on Paul Johnson and then explored those prior holdings of the Court that, he claimed, the majority had tacitly overruled. In the third part, he turned to what he called "the engine of discrimination we have finally completed."

A chief, perhaps the chief, conservative argument against affirmative action is that although the actual victims of discrimination should certainly be compensated and given some preference to make them whole, people who had not suffered from discrimination should not benefit from preferential plans. The Santa Clara plan, Scalia charged, did not remedy prior discrimination because there had been no prior sex discrimination to remedy. Rather, its stated goal had been all along to "mirror the racial and sexual composition of the entire county labor force," a statistical situation that would never occur in a truly discrimination-free world. To achieve that goal, the plan expected concrete results from its managers, and only through quotas could they achieve those results.

And who would pay for this plan? People like the petitioner, Paul Johnson, who had clearly and unfairly been discriminated against and denied a promotion he had fairly won. The majority, Scalia charged, glossed over the plain facts of the record that showed Johnson had had the better qualifications and ignored the testimony of Norman Graebner, as well as the finding of the district court, that gender had been the determining factor. Since the court of appeals had not rejected this finding as clearly erroneous, then under the federal rules he and the other justices had to accept them as true and not ignore them as the majority had done.

Scalia then accused the majority of ignoring the Court's earlier rulings, including the major case decided in the previous term, *Wygant v. Jackson Board of Education.* That case had made crystal clear that efforts to remedy social discrimination could not violate the Equal Protection Clause. Even though this case came up under Title VII, Scalia could not believe that Congress had intended to place a lesser restraint on discrimination by public agencies under the statute than existed under the Constitution. Only Justice O'Connor, in her concurrence, had attempted to explain away this incongruity, an effort that, however, had failed to convince him.

Scalia roamed over the entire gamut of the Court's earlier pronouncements and indicted the majority for its willful distortion of previous holdings or for ignoring them completely. Those cases had made plain that preferential programs had to be addressed to specific and egregious past or present discrimination, and that approach certainly had not been the case here. Instead, he charged, the majority had given its approval to a rank form of social engineering that had as its unrealistic and unattainable goal the reshaping of every work force to mirror the overall population. "It is absurd to think that the nationwide failure of road maintenance crews, for example, to achieve the

Agency's ambition of 36.4 percent female representation is attributable primarily, if even substantially, to systematic exclusion of women eager to shoulder pick and shovel."

Scalia noted that social attitudes that caused women to choose certain jobs and to avoid others could be "as nefarious as conscious, exclusionary discrimination." But whatever the truth or falsity of that assumption, no national consensus existed that even remotely compared to the general antipathy to conscious discrimination. The majority, he charged, had manipulated the law in an attempt to alter social attitudes, a direction sanctioned neither by statute nor by the Constitution.

In the last part of his eighteen-page draft, Scalia turned his guns on what he considered the chief culprit of the Court's consistent weakening of both Title VII and the Equal Protection Clause, the *Weber* opinion, and called for its reconsideration and overruling. Following Rehnquist's powerful dissent in *Weber*, Scalia charged that in that case the Court had completely rewritten the original intention of Title VII and distorted its true purpose of doing away with any and all forms of discrimination. In doing this, the Court had ignored the intent of Congress and had engaged in the most blatant form of judicial policymaking.

> In effect, *Weber* held that the legality of intentional discrimination by private employers against certain disfavored groups or individuals is to be judged not by Title VII but by a judicially crafted code of conduct, the contours of which are determined by no discernible standard, aside from . . . the divination of congressional "purposes" belied by the face of the statute and by its legislative history. We have been recasting that self-promulgated code of conduct ever since — and what it has led us to today adds to the reasons for abandoning it.

The latest decision of the Court, according to Scalia, went further than any previous decision, and not just in extending the *Weber* doctrine to public as well as to private employers. In effect, the majority opinion had taken the original meaning of Title VII, that forbade taking race or gender into account, and now required employers to do so. After today, he predicted, it would be "economic folly" for an employer not to engage in reverse discrimination, lest it be sued for

{ *Affirmative Action on Trial* }

failure to give preference to one minority or the other. "A statute designed to establish a color-blind and gender-blind workplace has thus been converted into a powerful engine of racism and sexism, not merely *permitting* intentional race- and sex-based discrimination, but often making it, through operation of the legal system, practically compelled." And who suffers? Innocent victims like Paul Johnson, "predominantly unknown, unaffluent, unorganized."

———

It was a powerful indictment, all the more so for the clarity in which Scalia had framed the issue. One could, of course, argue with Scalia's basic premises, that the Court had distorted the original meaning of Title VII, since in the Civil Rights Act of 1964 Congress had recognized the need for affirmative action programs to remedy past discrimination. And though some sections of the bill did seem to have been written with remarkable directness, other sections left a great deal to the imagination. Moreover, evidence — strong evidence — existed that the Court's interpretation of the "spirit" of Title VII, so derided by Scalia, had been right on target, that the Court had in fact understood it.

Statutory construction, that is, the Court's interpretation of a congressional law, is always open to review and revision by the Congress. On more than one occasion, Congress has revised a law in response to what it saw as judicial misinterpretation. If *Weber* and its progeny had been misguided, Congress could easily have stepped in and revised Title VII, in essence telling the Court, "You guys got it wrong. *This* is what we meant." The failure of Congress to do so can, by this reading, be taken as an endorsement of the *Weber* position.

Brennan recognized that at least some of Scalia's charges had to be refuted, lest he lose O'Connor, Powell, or both, and with them his majority. Two days after receiving the draft dissent, he circulated proposed revisions to his own opinion answering the more important points Scalia had raised. Most of the response he cast in the form of footnotes, both to downplay their importance and to keep his opinion on a positive track, rather than having it appear defensive.

He argued that Scalia had mistakenly equated Title VII and equal protection obligations. The Court had examined that issue and rejected the notion in *Weber* because the two derived from different portions of the Constitution. Title VII, originally focused on private employers, derived its authority from the Commerce Clause, and when Congress added public employers in 1972 it subjected them to the same criteria as it had originally applied to private firms. Although a public employer also had to satisfy the Constitution, that constituted a separate issue from Title VII and involved different standards.

Brennan also took issue with the charge that the Court had rewritten Title VII. The legislative history of the Civil Rights Act showed clearly, he claimed, that Congress had in fact wanted to give employers flexibility to devise programs aimed at remedying discrimination. He went on to remind the reader of the circumstances surrounding passage of the bill, the widespread racial unrest of the time to which businesses had begun to respond through early affirmative action plans.

Scalia had raised one issue that Brennan knew greatly bothered Sandra O'Connor, the predicate necessary to justify an affirmative action program. Scalia (and the Reagan administration) believed that an employer could institute a plan only to redress its own past discrimination. According to Brennan, the Court had specifically rejected that view, because it placed the employer on the horns of a cruel dilemma. Admit discrimination to justify affirmative action and be open to Title VII lawsuits, or deny past discrimination and be foreclosed from instituting affirmative action plans that might be wholly justified by the record. To buttress his argument, he quoted from O'Connor's concurrence in *Wygant* that made just this point.

Finally, Brennan dismissed Scalia's dire prediction that the ruling would loose a flood of "less qualified" minorities and women upon the work force, as employers sought to forestall possible Title VII liability, as well as Scalia's claim that Joyce had been less qualified than Johnson. Brennan defended the county's plan as consistent with standard personnel practices, in which the person with the highest score is not always chosen since there has to be flexibility to take other factors into account.

Only Lewis Powell responded to this memorandum and gently suggested that Brennan delete some of the references to the racial disorders at the time when Congress had been debating the 1964 Civil Rights Act. The discussion, Powell said, "based as it is on newspaper references, seems unnecessary and I think it may detract from the strength and persuasiveness of your excellent Court opinion."

He also wanted the opinion to make clear that *Johnson* did not override the *Wygant* holding that social discrimination by itself justified a plan using racial (or gender) classification. In response to Scalia's argument that nondiscriminatory reasons might account for women not working on road crews, Brennan, who had himself written quite eloquently on the prejudicial effects that stereotypes had on women, had again quoted from an O'Connor opinion. Discrimination, she had argued, creates assumptions about the "proper" employment for women, and the acceptance of these assumptions by women themselves produces a "self-fulfilling prophecy." To Powell, this ran too close to allowing general social discrimination as a rationale for a preferential plan.

The always courteous Virginian concluded with a note of appreciation for Brennan's work. "Thank you so much, Bill, for your attention to my concerns. This is another 'landmark' decision. You can well be proud of both this case and *Paradise.*"

Brennan recognized that Powell's suggestions made good sense; though he himself might be willing to permit an affirmative action plan in response to social discrimination, the key centrist votes on the Court shied away from such a stance. So he decided to eliminate the footnote completely and avoid the issue. He wrote to Powell the next day, February 28, to tell him he would accede to both requests. He also took the opportunity to express his appreciation.

"This letter," wrote Brennan, "is another opportunity to reiterate my pleasure in being able to work with you in this case to achieve a majority opinion for the Court. Thank you again, Lewis, for your comments and your patience."

Justice O'Connor, apparently stung by the bitterness in the Scalia dissent, revised her concurrence two more times, and in doing so edged closer to the dissenters, although in the end she still concurred in the result. O'Connor hinted that if the issue of overruling *Weber* had been raised, and if the case in the lower courts had involved equal protection claims, she might have voted differently. But in the end the statistical disparity, that "inexorable zero," convinced her that the county had sufficient justification to institute an affirmative action program. Scalia also made some revisions to his dissent, responding in part to Brennan's new points as well as to some of O'Connor's arguments.

On March 5, the reporter of decisions prepared a syllabus or headnote to be released with the opinion, summarizing the main points of the majority decision, and sent it to Brennan for his approval. The end was now rapidly approaching. On March 16, Brennan circulated his fifth and final draft; he still had a firm majority of five, with Sandra Day O'Connor concurring in the result. Chief Justice Rehnquist joined Scalia's dissent, and White subscribed to most of it.

Until 1971, many of the justices actually read their full opinions on decision days, although since the late 1930s some justices had adopted the practice of announcing the result and summarizing the reasoning. Chief Justice Burger finally convinced his colleagues that with the proliferation of opinions, the Court spent too much of its time reading aloud. Although individual justices may still, on occasion, read their dissents in order to draw attention, the general practice now is for the author of the majority opinion to announce the result, briefly summarize the reasoning, and note which justices have filed separate concurring or dissenting opinions. Full copies of all the opinions are available at the Clerk's Office on the day the decision is announced, but no advance notice is given of when a particular decision will be handed down.

Shortly after ten o'clock on Wednesday morning, March 25, 1987, six years after Paul Johnson had first filed his complaint in federal district court, Chief Justice Rehnquist declared that Justice Brennan would announce the Court's decision in No. 85-1129, *Johnson v. Transportation Agency, Santa Clara County, California*. Briefly and emotionlessly, Brennan informed the people in the courtroom that an affirmative action plan instituted by a public employer to remedy a statistical imbalance of women in its work force, even without a showing of prior discrimination, did not violate Title VII of the Civil Rights Act. The Santa Clara plan, therefore, remained in place. Diane Joyce had won.

CHAPTER 10

High Tide and Ebb

Following the Court's decision in *Johnson*, both friends and foes of preferential hiring plans interpreted it as a victory for affirmative action. The case, along with the *Paradise* decision handed down a few weeks earlier, seemed to cap a nine-year cycle, beginning with *Bakke*, that legitimized the use of race and gender to compensate for past discrimination. Although the Court had set some limits on preferential hiring, the central idea of affirmative action apparently had come through the ordeal of judicial scrutiny intact. Yet within a relatively short time, the certainty that had accompanied *Johnson* had all but disappeared.

On hearing the decision, an elated Diane Joyce initially responded with uncharacteristic restraint. "I knew I could do the job from the beginning," she told the Associated Press. "I knew I could do it very well. The case will have an impact on all women, and I'm very happy for them." A few days later, when the news had sunk in, she crowed with victory. "There was never any doubt in my mind that I was going to bury the sucker." But, she added, "I'm not a heroine. I'm not a pioneer. I went in for the money. It was pure greed. I'm more a rugged individualist than a feminist." When someone asked whether she felt bad for Paul Johnson, Joyce remembered all the times she had been turned down for no reason other than that she was female. "Why should I feel guilty now?" she retorted. "I've already given up thirty years of big bucks."

Paul Johnson called the decision "a gross miscarriage of justice" and said he could not understand how "people with intelligence could rule this way." Two years later, interviewed at his home, he remained bitter. "It's pretty damn sad," he said. "These people are up there and the first thing they're supposed to do is defend the Constitution of the United States. I have lost a lot of respect for that Court."

"All the broad questions have now been answered," a joyful Richard Seymour announced. The head of the Lawyers' Committee for Civil Rights Under Law, which had filed an *amicus* brief on behalf of the county plan, believed the most important aspect of the decision is that "the kind of affirmative action that has been practiced by most employers in this country over the last decade has been upheld by the Supreme Court." *Business Week* agreed. "The great affirmative action debate of the 1980s is over," the journal declared. The decision "ended a nightmare that has been plaguing companies since the Reagan administration began trying to rein in affirmative action. . . . With the key legal issues settled, companies can view affirmative action as an opportunity rather than a burden." The U.S. Chamber of Commerce also breathed an audible sigh of relief. The chamber's counsel, Stephen Bokat, noted that employers could now be assured of the legality of their plans, and he hoped the Reagan administration would finally give up its efforts to undo affirmative action.

The administration, however, refused to concede defeat. Terry Eastland, the spokesman for the Justice Department, expressed disappointment "that the Court has departed from the moral principle of non-discrimination for all citizens that is the basis of our civil rights laws." Bruce Fein of the conservative Heritage Foundation also questioned the wisdom of the decision but called the ruling "the most significant . . . doctrinally since the Court started to confront things in *Bakke.*"

Some liberals suggested that the extreme view pushed by the administration may have backfired. William Goldstein of the NAACP Legal Defense Fund, with tongue partially in cheek, gave credit to the assistant attorney general, William Bradford Reynolds, who had been a vociferous critic of affirmative action. Reynolds "really helped us develop the law. I don't think it would be as strong today if it were not for the extreme actions taken by the Justice Department."

In magazines and law journals, commentators praised or damned the *Johnson* decision according to their views on affirmative action. The conservative *National Review* still considered affirmative action against the law, and "there being no National Association for the Protection of White Males, white males will bear the brunt of this discrimination, with the Court's blessing." As if in response, the *New Republic* columnist TRB declared, "It's hard to feel any terrible injustice was done to Paul Johnson because he 'scored' two points higher on his interview." Though Scalia's dissent on the face of it seemed to make some sense, in the call for a color-blind, gender-blind legal standard, a closer reading showed that Scalia and other conservatives had a different agenda. "They want less civil rights, not more civil rights," TRB charged, "and should stop pretending otherwise."

Some feminist scholars charged that both the majority and its critics had failed to understand the issue. Giving Diane Joyce an edge over Paul Johnson, Chicago law professor Mary Becker wrote, would be affirmative action only if the two had been similarly situated. But, she claimed,

> The notion that they might have been similarly situated is fanciful. Their prior employment experiences were not similar even when they had identical titles. For Joyce, work as the only female road maintenance worker would have involved a constant struggle, including dealing with hazing and harassment. Johnson was one of the boys. It is, however, likely that many male decision makers would neither see what Joyce went through nor appreciate that her unique experiences might be qualifications for promotion.

In fact, Professor Becker claimed, men would probably see Johnson as more qualified because as a road dispatcher, Joyce would continue to have problems operating in a male world.

From a legal standpoint, the *Johnson* decision extended doctrines that the Court had been developing for nearly a decade. Most important, it gave public employers the same opportunity to institute affirmative action plans as private employers had and held them to the same standards under Title VII. Because the equal protection claim had not been litigated in the lower courts, the question remained whether an affirmative action plan by a public employer, challenged explicitly under the Fourteenth Amendment, would survive a legal challenge.

Second, the Court for the first time included women as a group eligible for affirmative action. Although it seemed logical to extend to women the reasoning that had informed the Court's previous decisions on race-based preferential programs, no one had been sure if in fact the Court itself would take that step. Some feminists also worried that because race and gender discrimination derived from different causes, a simple extension of *Bakke* might actually work against women. *Johnson* not only explicitly allowed a gender-based plan, it also gave the employer a great deal of flexibility in determining the need for such a plan and its details.

The third important aspect of the decision involved the factual predicate that the majority had adopted. For Justice O'Connor, the "inexorable zero" provided sufficient proof that women had been kept out of the job category, and statistics, without proof of actual prior discrimination, seemed sufficient to justify instituting a plan.

The approval of public employer plans, the extension of the legal concept justifying affirmative action to women, and the flexibility in fashioning the program certainly seemed to warrant optimistic claims that affirmative action had finally been fully accepted, by the courts as well as by the business community.

Not everyone, of course, shared this euphoric outlook. Conservatives still opposed what they labeled as "quotas" and "reverse discrimination" and demanded that if the United States wanted to do away with bias in employment, then it should apply the same color-blind and gender-blind standards to everyone. Feminist legal scholars pointed out that women still did not share the same protected position as blacks, and programs that either implicitly or explicitly discriminated against women did not face the same strict scrutiny barriers as those involving race.

Moreover, the Court's decisions on affirmative action really said little more than Justice Powell had said in *Bakke*, that under certain circumstances, it might be legitimate to take race, and now gender, into account in employment decisions in an effort to remedy past discrimination. Although the Court's approval obviously meant a great deal, especially to employers seeking to protect themselves from future lawsuits, these decisions have not resolved many of the truly difficult questions surrounding affirmative action.

It is one thing to say that blacks or women have been discriminated against, but what other classes should come under the umbrella? And how does one define the class of "innocent victims" whose interests, according to *Johnson* as well as to *Weber*, are not to be "needlessly trammeled upon." How, also, especially in promotion decisions, can one define with any clarity the "best qualified" standard? In Paul Johnson's case, the two-point spread in the test score certainly did not make him better qualified than Diane Joyce, but what about the judgment of his superiors? Though one cannot objectify such judgments, they are certainly important, and from the supervisory point of view, critical in promotion decisions.

These are unresolved *legal* questions, yet they are also unresolved issues of public policy. A quarter-century after Lyndon Johnson called for affirmative action, the country seemed no closer to agreeing on whether there should be such plans, and if so, what criteria should be applied. Who should be helped? How much should they be helped? And, in an era of limited resources, who would pay? Paul Johnson put the issue succinctly: "If they're going to make a change, why should I be the goat? If they want to do it, let them compensate me."

––––––

Both critics and champions of the Court's decisions have noted that the justices had not been unanimous in a single one of the affirmative action cases. Many had been decided by a 5-to-4 vote, and even the 6-to-3 tally in *Johnson* did not indicate an impressive consensus. Sandra Day O'Connor had concurred in the result, not in the reasoning, and had indicated that if faced by an equal protection claim and a direct challenge to *Weber*, she might well vote the other way. That left a bare majority of five, and one of them, Lewis Powell, did not support all affirmative action plans. So only four members of the Court — the four oldest members — could be counted on in future cases.

Then at the close of the term, Lewis Powell resigned after a distinguished fifteen-year career on the bench. He had had some serious health problems, and while apparently recovered, he worried about how a recurrent illness or even death might affect the Court. Moreover, if he waited another year, the president would be naming a successor in the middle of an election campaign, and Powell did not want to see the Court embroiled in campaign politics. Ronald Reagan's nomination of court of appeals judge Robert Bork, however, touched off the most bitter confirmation struggle of this century and triggered an extensive public debate on many of the Court's recent doctrines, such as affirmative action. Although liberals managed to defeat Bork, the man who ultimately took Lewis Powell's seat on the Court, Ninth Circuit Judge Anthony Kennedy, stood firmly aligned with the conservative bloc.

The October 1987 term did not have any significant affirmative action cases on the docket. Moreover, in a case that might have implications for future affirmative action suits, a unanimous bench held that a former bank employee could use statistics to prove she had been the victim of racial discrimination in the bank's promotion practices (*Watson v. Fort Worth Bank & Trust Co.* [1988]). The Court brushed aside a brief by the Reagan administration opposing the use of statistics to prove racial or gender discrimination and cleared the way for plaintiffs in employment discrimination suits to introduce the number of blacks or women at management levels as evidence of bias.

Then in the 1988 term, the roof seemed to fall in on affirmative action in the high court. First the Court backtracked on nearly two decades of precedent regarding the use of statistics to demonstrate bias. Ever since the *Griggs* case in 1971, the Court had permitted statistical evidence of a racial imbalance — the same types of statistics involved in the *Johnson* case — to support a charge of discrimination under Title VII, even if the hiring practices appeared facially neutral. Given an imbalance, the employer then had the burden of proving that the practices that had created the imbalance were justified by the circumstances of the business.

By a 5-to-4 vote *(Wards Cove Packing Co. v. Antonio)*, the Court gave companies accused of discrimination an important procedural victory by shifting the burden of proof from the employer to the employee alleging discrimination. Moreover, in the opinion written by Justice White, employees could no longer use statistics of racial disparity in the workplace to support charges of discrimination. In a biting dissent, Justice Blackmun questioned whether the majority "still believes that race discrimination . . . is a problem in our society, or even remembers that it ever was."

The Court further restricted Title VII suits when it narrowly construed the law's time limitations. The majority held that suits charging facially neutral seniority systems with discriminatory impact had to be filed at the time the system is adopted, not when its operation subsequently has allegedly discriminatory effects. Since it might be impossible to know how a system would operate at its inception, this ruling could all but eliminate Title VII suits against seniority plans (*Lorance v. AT&T Technologies, Inc.*).

The Court dealt two potentially devastating blows against affirmative action plans. The first case, *Martin v. Wilks*, involved an archetypical consent decree in Birmingham, Alabama. In response to a discrimination suit by blacks against the city, a federal district court had approved two consent decrees in which the city agreed to hire more black firefighters and to arrange promotion goals for blacks. The court also ruled efforts by a white firefighters' union as well as some individual white firemen to intervene in the case as untimely.

A group of other white firemen, who had not been involved in the earlier suit, then sued the city under Title VII, claiming that they had been denied promotions in favor of less-qualified blacks. The city admitted that it had made race-conscious decisions but argued as a defense that such decisions had been permitted, indeed required, as part of the consent decree, and therefore it was immune to this type of attack.

The court of appeals for the Eighth Circuit, as well as a majority of the Supreme Court, disagreed. Justice Rehnquist rejected the idea of an "impermissible collateral attack" that would protect consent decrees from suits by persons not party to the agreement. A person, the chief justice declared, cannot be deprived of his legal rights in a proceeding to which he is not a party.

The decision raised alarms throughout the nation in cities that had signed consent decrees in response to antidiscrimination suits. In nearly all such agreements, there are many people who are not parties to the agreement who may be affected by its terms. Under this ruling, any such person could attack the decrees as impinging on his or her rights and then tie up the municipal government for years in expensive and time-consuming litigation.

The decision that posed the greatest threat to affirmative action came in a case challenging a minority set-aside program adopted by the city of Richmond, Virginia. Congress had first adopted set-aside programs in 1980, when it had determined the existence of long-term and widespread discrimination in the construction industry. It had therefore required that prime contractors subcontract 10 percent of

federally financed construction projects to minority business enter-
prises (MBEs), which it statutorily defined as any business at least 51
percent owned by blacks, Spanish-speaking, Orientals, Indians, Eskimos, or Aleuts. The Court had upheld the federal set-aside in *Fullilove
v. Klutznik* (1980), ruling that Congress had sufficient evidence to
support its findings of discrimination and ample power under the
Fourteenth Amendment to enact such remedial legislation.

Following that decision, many state and local governments en-
acted similar set-aside measures designed to support MBEs. In 1983,
Richmond, Virginia, which is 50 percent black, approved a program
calling for at least 30 percent of all city-financed prime contracts to go
to MBEs and adopted the same definitions used by Congress. The
city council developed no evidence that discrimination existed in the
area construction industry other than noting that few blacks belonged
to the local employer trade groups. The one bit of hard evidence
showed that over the previous five years, MBEs had received only
0.67 percent of the city's prime contracts.

The J. A. Croson Company, attempting to bid on a city contract to
install new plumbing fixtures in the jail, could not find an MBE willing and able to enter a bid for the subcontract. When the city rejected
all bids and announced it would rebid the contract, the Croson Company sued, charging reverse discrimination.

In *Richmond v. J. A. Croson Co.* (1989) Justice O'Connor, for a
6-to-3 majority, held that the city had not proven its case that prior
discrimination existed and that its 30 percent figure bore no relation
to any of the facts submitted in support of the set-aside. "An amor-
phous claim that there has been past discrimination in a particular
industry cannot justify the use of an unyielding racial quota." She also
held that such programs, when undertaken by state or local agencies,
are subject to a strict scrutiny standard, the highest criterion used by
the courts in racial classification cases.

The majority opinion distinguished between the power of Congress in this area, which derives directly from the Fourteenth Amendment, and that of lesser governmental agencies, which do not enjoy
such constitutional grants. O'Connor did not hold that state and local
governments can never establish set-aside programs; she carefully
spelled out what proofs they had to offer and what standards they had
to meet. One had to establish the existence of prior discrimination

and then narrowly tailor the program to meet the specific situation. The Richmond program failed to meet any of these criteria.

The National League of Cities found the ruling "troubling in what it says about the capacity of states and cities to govern at all in some matters." The decision did not, however, nullify congressional set-aside measures, nor those voluntarily undertaken by private firms. Moreover, though it might be more difficult in the future for cities and states to establish the evidentiary threshold, it would not be impossible. Parren Mitchell, chairman of the Minority Business Enterprise Legal Defense Fund, believed evidence exists to support findings of extensive discrimination in construction and other industries and that it would be a starting point for future successful programs. By this interpretation, the Court did not attack set-asides; Richmond merely failed to set up its program properly.

In some ways, these cases did no more than tighten up some of the protections the Court had established earlier; in other ways, they seemed clear evidence of a definite turn to the right. Conservatives quickly grasped at the latter interpretation. "For the first time in thirty years," exclaimed Bruce Fein, "the Court has a working five-member majority saying that the goal is color blindness and gender blindness." Walter Burns of the American Enterprise Institute noted that the civil rights community had launched its campaign against Robert Bork because it had feared he would champion just such a path. "Now they are getting what they feared, without him on the Court."

Although Congress in the 1991 Civil Rights Act reversed some of the Court's statutory rulings, and although the justices approved a Federal Communications Commission (FCC) set-aside program reserving a certain number of frequencies for minority station owners (*Metro Broadcasting, Inc. v. FCC*), both the Court and the country seemed to bear out the conservative prophecy that the era of affirmative action was over. In *Shaw v. Reno* (1993) the Court, by a 5-to-4 vote, raised the possibility that election districts gerrymandered to give minorities representation, a procedure blessed by the Voting Rights Act, might be unconstitutional.

Then in the most important affirmative action case since *Johnson*, a 5-to-4 Court overturned both *Fullilove* and *Metro Broadcasting*. In *Fullilove* the Court had indicated that Congress had the power under the enforcement provision of the Fourteenth Amendment to establish set-aside programs solely on its factual finding of prior racial discrimination. In *Adarand Constructors, Inc. v. Pena* (1995), Justice O'Connor, speaking for a highly splintered Court, held that under the Fifth and Fourteenth Amendments' Due Process Clauses, any action involving racial classification, including set-asides, by either the states or the federal government, would be judged by a standard of strict scrutiny. Just as the courts have frowned on measures that discriminate on the basis of race, so now they would frown on those that favored on the basis of race. O'Connor made it clear that this did not mean that all affirmative action programs were automatically unconstitutional; rather, the government would have to show a record of actual prior discrimination in order to justify a narrowly tailored plan.

———

The *Adarand* decision came in the midst of a growing national debate on affirmative action, one that had indeed turned ugly. The economic downturn in the early 1990s saw many American companies downsize their payrolls, and other firms moved manufacturing operations to Latin America and Asia to take advantage of cheaper labor. White males believed that in the competition for remaining jobs, affirmative action plans would put them at a disadvantage against women and minority applicants. Jesse Helms shamelessly took advantage of this fear in his 1990 campaign for reelection as one of North Carolina's senators. His media adviser, Carter Wrenn, produced a notorious ad showing white hands crumpling a job-rejection letter while the voice-over explained that a minority applicant had been hired even though the white applicant had better qualifications.

Republicans in their drive to capture the House and Senate in the 1994 midterm elections pulled out the throttle to full in their attack on affirmative action. President Bill Clinton had to admit that in some instances affirmative action plans had not worked as well as one might have wished, but his plea to mend the system rather than discard it found little favor among white male blue-collar workers. Then in summer 1995, at the urging of Gov. Pete Wilson (who hoped that he might be able to ride the affirmative action issue to the Republican presidential nomination), the Board of Regents of the University of

California — the same system that produced the *Bakke* case — voted to end thirty years of effort to bring more minority students into California's institutions of higher education.

One could not miss the growing conservatism among the country's voters, especially the male blue-collar workers who rallied to Pat Buchanan's campaign for the Republican presidential nomination, but the chorus against affirmative action also found echoes among academics, who pronounced the programs ineffective, and black conservatives, led by Thomas Sowell, who pronounced racial preference plans demeaning to African-Americans and other minorities.

Affirmative action has been debated in this country for well over a quarter-century. There are individuals who believe that only preferential plans will abolish the legacy of racism and sexism in this country; others take just the opposite view, that affirmative action indeed perpetuates race and gender bias and stereotypes. Probably the large majority of Americans believe that there ought to be some help given to the people directly affected by discrimination, and even to blacks and women in general. The consensus breaks down when one begins to look at specific issues, such as goals versus quotas, recruitment versus promotion, and who pays for the program in terms of lost or closed opportunities.

There is also a question of whether, aside from some individual success stories, affirmative action has been an effective policy. Statistics hardly prove the case one way or the other; on the one hand, the black middle class seems larger than ever, and one can find blacks, women, and Hispanics in many middle-management and professional positions. On the other hand, some studies indicate that the top jobs remain disproportionately in the hands of white males, and during the Reagan years, blacks and women apparently suffered significant slippage. In a study of affluent Westchester County, New York, white males held two out of every three of the 487 county government jobs paying $43,000 or more, although they made up barely one-third of the total work force of 8,500 people. In 1984, women had held 30 percent of those jobs, and blacks 8.7 percent; four years later their numbers had slipped to 25.5 and 7.1 percent. Another study, involving blacks in journalism, showed not only that blacks were underrepresented in proportion to their numbers in the general population but also that the number of blacks working in televised news had declined 13 percent from 1979 to 1986. In the most recent survey of the status of blacks in America, researchers concluded:

> The status of black Americans today can be characterized as a glass that is half full — if measured by the progress since 1939 — or as a glass that is half empty — if measured by the persisting disparities between black and white Americans since the early 1970s. . . . Since the early 1970s, the economic status of blacks relative to whites has, on average, stagnated or deteriorated.

In a section devoted to affirmative action, the report documents not only the continuing discrimination faced by blacks but also the failure of affirmative action. In 1984, the last year for which figures are available, the average yearly earnings of black male college graduates, a group most likely to benefit from affirmative action, amounted to only 74 percent of their white counterparts. Between 1970 and 1986, the proportion of black families with inflation-adjusted incomes of $35,000 or more increased only 4 percent, from 18 to 22 percent. A worse story unfolds when one looks at blue-collar black workers, where in some categories real income *decreased* by 20 percent in the affluent eighties. All in all, black per capita income stood at 57 percent of the white level in 1984, exactly the same percentage it had been in 1971.

The story is somewhat different, and better, for women, especially white women who have sought to enter the professions. In some law schools, for example, recent classes have run at almost an identical gender mix as that of society at large. It is clear that there are more women doctors, lawyers, judges, and business executives. Today over 15 percent of doctors and lawyers are women, as compared with less than 3 percent in 1970. During the Reagan years, despite the administration's opposition to affirmative action, women's wages did increase; in 1987, for the first time, the hourly earnings of women employed full-time exceeded 75 percent of the earnings of men working full-time and with the same amount of schooling, up from the 60 percent figure that held fairly steady throughout the 1970s. Some economists suggest that unless and until the United States adopts either a comprehensive family support system or imposes wage controls, it is unlikely that women overall will ever earn as much as men, because of the time they drop out of the labor market to have families.

Like their black counterparts, women in blue-collar or so-called pink collar clerical jobs have shared least in the economic good times. Though some estimates place women at nearly half of the professional work force (including business management), they are still for the most part excluded from skilled crafts. Only 8.6 percent of precision, production, crafts, and repair jobs are held by women; only 3 percent of mechanics are female, and 1.5 percent of construction workers. Despite Justice Scalia's assumption that women do not want to go into these traditional male domains, the evidence shows that they do but that they also recognize the barriers. When Santa Clara County surveyed 100 of its female employees in 1984, it found that eighty-five of them did in fact want to work in the skilled-craft categories, which paid twice or three times a secretary's wages. Ninety of them said they knew they would not be able to get those jobs because of discrimination!

———

Four decades after the Supreme Court decided *Brown v. Board of Education* and thirty years after Congress passed the historic Civil Rights and Voting Rights Acts, there is little question that the mood of the country has shifted significantly. A Time/CNN poll in early 1995 found that 77 percent of the people surveyed believed that affirmative action programs frequently discriminate against whites; even 66 percent of the black respondents answered the same way.

The legal future of affirmative action is questionable, though, thanks to a 1996 decision in the U.S. Court of Appeals for the Fifth Circuit, which struck down the University of Texas affirmative action plan that favored black and Hispanic minorities. In *Hopwood v. Texas*, the court told the University of Texas law school that it could not use admission standards for minority students different from those it used for white students, a ruling that appeared to run contrary to *Bakke*. The university then appealed to the Supreme Court, which denied cert, and thus left the Fifth Circuit decision in place.

Although the *Hopwood* decision technically applies only in the Fifth Circuit, the high court's seeming approval of it will force schools all over the country to reexamine their affirmative action policies. Contrary to the claims of some, *Hopwood* does not negate all affirmative action plans. In *Bakke*, Justice Powell did not say that schools could use different standards (as Texas was doing) but only that race could be a factor in making decisions about employment and admissions. If two candidates for a job or for admission to graduate school both have roughly equal qualifications, then race can still be a factor.

Moreover, in many businesses and schools that once discriminated, affirmative action is not only well established, but it has also been successful in the way such plans were intended to be. At present these plants have a mixed work force and these colleges have a diverse student body. Since minorities know that they will be considered at these places, they apply in sufficient numbers so that employers and admissions officers do, in fact, have large pools of applicants that do include well-qualified minorities. That is how affirmative action was always intended to work.

The story started with Paul Johnson, Diane Joyce, and the Santa Clara County Transportation Agency, and it ends with them as well. Johnson, bitter after the Ninth Circuit reversed Judge Ingram, took early retirement at the end of 1984. He and his wife Betty moved to the small seaside town of Sequim, on Washington's Olympic Peninsula. He felt, with some justification, that the press had made him the "heavy" of this story and several times during our interview said how tired he was of the distortions and wanted only to see the facts set out clearly. He often got calls from other people involved in reverse discrimination suits, and in 1989 he sent out an "Open Letter to the White Males of America," suggesting that they should somehow organize before any more of their rights were taken away.

James Dawson, who argued Johnson's case in the district and appeals court, left the office where Johnson met him and formed his own law partnership, which later merged with another to form a larger firm. Dawson continues to practice law in San Jose.

Constance Brooks left Mountain States about a year after the case and is now a partner in the Portland, Oregon, law firm of Lindsay, Hart, Neil & Weigler. A good part of her practice involves public interest questions.

With the end of the Reagan administration, Charles Fried returned to the Harvard Law School, from which he occasionally sallies forth to argue cases, as a private lawyer, before the Supreme Court.

Steven Woodside has remained with Santa Clara County but has been promoted, and he is now chief county counsel. David Rosenfeld, who represented the union, continues to practice in San Francisco.

Michael Baratz, who served as director for Local 715 of the Service Employees International Union and who championed Diane Joyce's cause, is now in Washington, D.C., the director of Field Services and Bargaining for the international union. His place in San Jose has been taken by Kristy Sermersheim, who spoke up for Joyce and stood by her during the protracted legal proceedings.

Has anything really changed in the Transportation Agency because of the suit and the affirmative action plan that caused it? On this issue there seems to be general agreement: things are generally the same as they were in the early eighties. There are a few more minorities, a few more women, but as Michael Baratz said, "The guys are still the same today; by and large the same culture exists." Kristy Sermersheim agreed; things have not changed, and the road department remains predominantly white, predominantly male.

Suzanne Wilson is still a supervisor, and she takes a far more optimistic view. Reform takes time, she says, but the longer the affirmative action plan is in place, the more things will open up. There have been some incremental changes, and as the old guard managers retire or move on, they will be replaced, sometimes by women or minorities, but certainly by people sensitive to the problems faced by women and minorities.

Diane Joyce has the dispatcher's mike but still feels the resentment of many of her male co-workers. She does not really expect that she will see revolutionary changes in her lifetime, but she has hopes for the future. There are now other women—a few—working on the road crews, including her daughter Donna.

A few years after the Supreme Court ruled in her favor, she applied for, but did not get, a job as assistant road district superintendent in neighboring Monterey County. "They accepted my application," she noted, "and they didn't say they wanted a man. Now, for me, that's progress."

On November 5, 1996, California provided the first opportunity for an at-large electorate to express its views on affirmative action. California is not only the largest state in the Union, it is also the most racially and ethnically diverse with significant Asian, Hispanic, and African-American populations. It is the state that began the legal controversy over affirmative action in the *Bakke* case and was, of course, the setting for *Johnson*. Probably no other state went to such lengths to establish affirmative action plans, and conversely, no state has had as many lawsuits involving affirmative action.

Because of the state's diversity, affirmative action tended not only to redress imbalances but to create new ones. According to a Pacific Research Institute study of the state's civil service since 1976, using the relevant work-force criteria mandated by the Supreme Court, blacks who were already overrepresented in the civil service increased their proportion by 132 percent, while the number of whites decreased by 63 percent. The study found that if strict proportionality had been enforced, blacks would have lost 10,362 state jobs, Filipinos 3,606, and women, 7,413; the "winners" in job reapportionment would have been white males, who made up only one-fourth of the state's work force.

Resentment against what some people perceived to be quotas benefiting everyone but whites led two scholars, Glynn Custred and Thomas Wood, to come up with a ballot initiative entitled Proposition 209. Its key section read, "The state shall not discriminate against, or grant preferential treatment to, any individual or group on the basis of race, sex, color, ethnicity, or national origin in the operation of public employment, public education, or public contracting." Custred and Wood had no problem collecting sufficient signatures to put the initiative on the fall ballot. Although Governor Pete Wilson of California campaigned strenuously on its behalf, President Clinton and Senator Dole, both of whom made numerous trips to California, studiously ignored the issue.

The campaign over Propostion 209 was vicious. One group enlisted Ku Klux Klansman David Duke of Louisiana to debate civil rights activist Joe Hicks, and opponents of Proposition 209 subsequently plastered the state with ads charging that the Klan supported the initiative. Actress Christine Lahti told a rally that if 209 passed, it would set the cause of women back twenty-five years. Supporters of 209 countered that its language was the same as that used by Lyndon Johnson, Hubert Humphrey, Martin Luther King, Jr., and the 1964 Civil Rights Act.

On Election Day, California voters approved Proposition 209 by a 54 to 46 margin, and both sides immediately filed lawsuits; opponents to block the state from ending existing affirmative action plans, and supporters to require the state to implement 209 at once. As one commentator noted, courts rarely overturn ballot initiatives unless they clearly conflict with the federal Constitution but often meliorate their impact. Assuming this observation to be true, affirmative action in California would be cut back but not necessarily eliminated. Despite claims about the "mandate" of the vote, it is far from clear what the California electorate's approval of Proposition 209 specifically means. Certainly, Republican strategists who look at the polling results should be wary of recommending that their candidates go all out against affirmative action. Exit polls showed that whites in general supported Proposition 209 by a 60 to 40 margin, and that black men opposed it 3 to 1. Women were evenly divided in their vote, but within this group white women supported the proposition 57 to 43. In terms of age, the strongest supporters of 209 were voters over 60. Those in the 18 to 29 age bracket opposed it 47 to 53, the 30 to 44 age group was divided evenly, and voters aged 45 to 59 supported it by a 55 to 45 margin. Among ethnic groups, Asians opposed the proposition by only a 45 to 55 margin, far less than other minority groups.

Comparing these figures to the presidential vote, Clinton's biggest support came from voters aged 18 to 29 (57%) and from those over 60 (55%), the two groups most at odds over Proposition 209. Blacks and Hispanics gave Clinton an overwhelming percentage of their votes (84% and 72% respectively), whereas whites chose Clinton over Dole by 46 to 42, and Asians by 53 to 42. Even in income distribution, Clinton took every group except those earning more than $100,000 annually. Every one of these income groups, with the exception of those earning less than $15,000 a year, voted in favor of 209.

Looking at Proposition 209 as a referendum on the future of affirmative action, if only in California, it is difficult to understand what voters want — certainly not quotas, which unfortunately a number of state agencies have put into place. (At the time of the vote, the state tax office planned to hire 95 male typists and 45 white typists, in order to rectify perceived imbalances in their work force.) Even without establishing quotas, the state has the ability to seek out talented capable workers and students from all groups. At this time, there are enough minority and female workers, many of whom are in supervisory positions, to ensure an end to the type of "good old boy" network that characterized the Santa Clara highway department.

The proposition does not affect private employers, except those with state contracts, and initial reports indicate that many of the state's largest employers have no plans to dismantle their affirmative action programs. First, to do so could result in violating parts of the 1964 Civil Rights Act; and second, unless there is a compelling reason (which 209 is not), companies would just as soon not "fix something that ain't broken." In a state such as California with a diverse population, employers want the ethnic composition of their companies to represent the people they serve. They do not want to lose female, black, Hispanic, or Asian customers who may be offended by an all-white, all-male company work force.

Proposition 209 is not the last word on affirmative action, even in California. It will be a long time before the dust of lawsuits has settled and new plans have been implemented. There is no consensus on the national level other than that people are opposed to quotas. In the end, programs, lawsuits, and debates come down to people like Paul Johnson and Diane Joyce, whose lives are affected directly, for better or worse, by affirmative action.

The prime sources for this book are the records and briefs in the *Johnson v. Santa Clara* case at the three levels at which it was heard, the district court, the Ninth Circuit, and the U.S. Supreme Court. The transcript of the trial in the district court is key to this story, since witnesses on both sides confirmed the basic facts of the case. Parts of the transcript, as well as Judge William A. Ingram's findings of fact and law, are included in the record attached to the briefs in the high court. The decision of the Ninth Circuit can be found at 748 F.2d 1308 (9th Cir. 1984); the Supreme Court decision is at 480 U.S. 616 (1987).

Justice William Brennan kindly allowed me to examine his office files on this case, although as a sitting justice at the time he could not discuss it. The file included not only the various drafts of his opinions and the notes from other justices but also memorandums on the conferences at which certiorari had been granted and the case decided. Since then his files have been deposited in the Manuscript Division of the Library of Congress. One of his clerks that year, Mitt Regan, Jr., now at the Georgetown University Law Center, confirmed details of how Brennan's chambers handled cases.

In this book I rely, far more than is usual, on oral history interviews with participants. It is not that their stories provided the factual basis but that I was able to understand far better the environment in which the events unfolded, the attitudes of the male workers in the road division, the difficulties women faced in trying to gain equal opportunities, and the problems confronted by lawyers handling these cases. Steven Woodside was amazing, and he spent several hours with me, including going over the transcript of the oral argument before the Supreme Court explaining who had asked which question, what they were trying to get at, and his strategy in answering. Even my son, who had adopted a rather skeptical attitude toward some of these participants, later admitted how impressed he had been. We interviewed James Dawson in his office in San Jose and met Connie Brooks for a lengthy and delicious dinner in San Francisco's Chinatown, where we heard her story of preparation. Steve, Jim, and Connie recognized and praised the abilities of the other attorneys, and judging from the tape of the oral argument, it is clear that the clients in this case could not have asked for better legal representation.

The two central interviews, of course, were with Paul Johnson and his wife in their home on Washington's Olympic Peninsula and with Diane Joyce in Santa Clara. They still felt quite passionate about their experience, and while I have tried to write as objective a book as possible, I hope some of their emotions about affirmative action and what they endured has come through. Other interviews were with Michael Baratz and Kristy Sermersheim of the union, and the union's attorney, David Rosenfeld; Suzanne Wilson of the county's Board of Supervisors; and former Solicitor General Charles Fried.

There have been numerous books written about affirmative action in general and on race in particular, and I have listed some of the more important ones, but there is nothing in book form on women and affirmative action. The student who wishes to examine affirmative action will do better to peruse the literally hundreds of articles in the popular press, especially the African-American and women's journals, to get some of the flavor of the high emotions triggered by the issue. Legal periodicals will also provide analysis of some of the constitutional and statutory questions in the various cases.

Among the books that I found particularly useful were Herman Belz, *Equality Transformed: A Quarter-Century of Affirmative Action* (New Brunswick, N.J.: Transaction Press, 1991); Anthony P. Carnevale and Susan Carol Stone, *The American Mosaic* (New York: McGraw-Hill, 1995); Stephen L. Carter, *Reflections of an Affirmative Action Baby* (New York: Basic Books, 1991); Susan D. Clayton and Faye J. Crosby, *Justice, Gender and Affirmative Action* (Ann Arbor: University of Michigan Press, 1992); Carl Cohen, *Naked Racial Preference* (Latham, Md.: Madison Books, 1995); John Edwards, *When Race Counts: The Morality of Racial Preference in Britain and America* (London and New York: Routledge, 1995); Susan Faludi, *Backlash: The Undeclared War Against American Women* (New York: Crown, 1991); Ronald J. Fiscus, *The Constitutional Logic of Affirmative Action*, ed. Stephen Wasby (Durham, N.C.: Duke University Press, 1992); Nathan Glazer, *Affirmative Discrimination: Ethnic Inequality and Public Policy* (New York: Basic Books, 1975); Jonathan Kaufman, *Broken Alliance* (New York: Scribner's, 1988); Jonathan S. Leonard, *The Impact of Affirmative Action* (Washington, D.C.: Government Printing Office, 1983); and Frederick R. Lynch, *Invisible Victims: White Males and the Crisis of Affirmative Action* (New York: Greenwood, 1989).

See also Nicolaus Mills, ed., *Debating Affirmative Action* (New York: Delta, 1994); Bernard Schwartz, *Behind Bakke: Affirmative Action and the Supreme Court* (New York: NYU Press, 1988); Allan P. Sindler, *Bakke, DeFunis and Minority Admissions: The Quest for Equal Opportunity* (New York: Longmans, 1978); Thomas Sowell, *Affirmative Action Reconsidered: Was It Necessary in Academia?* (Washington, D.C.: American Enterprise Institute, 1975), *Civil Rights: Rhetoric or Reality?* (New York: Morrow, 1984), and *The Vision of the Anointed* (New York: Basic Books, 1995); Shelby Steele, *The Content of Our Character* (New York: St. Martin's, 1990); Stephen Steinberg, *Turning Back: The Retreat from Racial Justice in American Thought and Policy* (Boston: Beacon Press, 1995); J. Harvie Wilkinson III, *From Brown to Bakke: The Supreme Court and School Integration, 1954–1978* (New York: Oxford University Press, 1979); Steven Yates, *Civil Wrongs: What Went Wrong with Affirmative Action* (San Francisco: Institute for Contemporary Studies, 1994).

Adarand Constructors, Inc. v. Pena, 115 S.Ct. 2097 (1995)

Britton v. South Bend Community School Corp., 775 F.2d 794 (7th Cir. 1985)

Brown v. Board of Education, 347 U.S. 483 (1954)

California v. Webster, 430 U.S. 313 (1977)

California Federal Savings & Loan v. Guerra, 479 U.S. 272 (1987)

City of Los Angeles Dept. of Water v. Manhart, 435 U.S. 702 (1978)

Craig v. Boren, 429 U.S. 190 (1976)

DeFunis v. Odegaard, 416 U.S. 312 (1974)

Firefighters v. Cleveland, 478 U.S. 501 (1986)

Firefighters Local Union No. 1784 v. Stotts, 467 U.S. 561 (1984)

Frontiero v. Richardson, 411 U.S. 677 (1973)

Fullilove v. Klutznik, 448 U.S. 448 (1980)

General Electric Co. v. Gilbert, 429 U.S. 125 (1976)

Goesart v. Cleary, 335 U.S. 464 (1948)

Griggs v. Duke Power Co., 401 U.S. 424 (1971)

Hazelwood School District v. United States, 433 U.S. 299 (1977)

Hishon v. King & Spaulding, 467 U.S. 69 (1984)

Hopwood v. Texas, 84 F.3d 720 (5th Cir. 1996), cert. denied, 116 S.Ct. 2581 (1996)

Janowiak v. Corporate City of South Bend, 750 F.2d 557 (7th Cir. 1984)

Local 28 Sheet Metal Workers v. EEOC, 478 U.S. 421 (1986)

Lorance v. AT&T Technologies, Inc., 490 U.S. 900 (1989)

McDonald v. Sante Fe Trail Transportation Co., 427 U.S. 273 (1976)

McDonnell Douglas Corp. v. Green, 411 U.S. 792 (1973)

Martin v. Wilks, 490 U.S. 775 (1989)

Meritor Savings Bank v. Vinson, 477 U.S. 57 (1986)

Metro Broadcasting, Inc. v. FCC, 497 U.S. 547 (1990)

Newport News Shipbuilding & Drydock Company v. EEOC, 462 U.S. 669 (1983)

Reed v. Reed, 404 U.S. 71 (1971)

Regents of the University of California v. Bakke, 438 U.S. 265 (1978)

Richmond, Va. v. J.A. Croson Co., 488 U.S. 469 (1989)

Shaw v. Reno, 113 S.Ct. 2816 (1993)

Stanton v. Stanton, 421 U.S. 7 (1975)

United States v. Paradise, 480 U.S. 149 (1987)

U.S. Postal Service Board of Governors v. Aikens, 460 U.S. 711 (1983)

United Steelworkers of America v. Weber, 443 U.S. 193 (1979)

Wards Cove Packing Co. v. Antonio, 490 U.S. 642 (1989)

Watson v. Fort Worth Bank & Trust Co., 487 U.S. 977 (1988)

Wengler v. Druggists Mutual Insurance Co., 446 U.S. 142 (1980)

Wygant v. Jackson Board of Education, 476 U.S. 267 (1986)

CHRONOLOGY

JOHNSON V. TRANSPORTATION AGENCY, SANTA CLARA COUNTY, CALIFORNIA
DOCKET NO. 85-1129

1964	Civil Rights Act becomes law. Its Title VII provision bans employment discrimination based on "race, color, sex, or national origin."
1965, 1967	President Lyndon Johnson issues Executive Orders 11246 and 11375, requiring federal contractors to take "affirmative action" to recruit, hire, and promote more minorities and women.
1971	President Richard Nixon unveils Philadelphia Plan, establishing goals, timetables, and enforcement procedures for federal affirmative action programs.
1972	Equal Employment Opportunity Act expands affirmative action to include state and local as well as federal hiring procedures.
1974	Paul Johnson and Diane Joyce apply for East Yard dispatcher's job in Santa Clara County's Transportation Agency. Neither is hired. Joyce is told she needs road crew experience, which she obtains over the next five years.
1978	The Supreme Court's 5-to-4 decision in *Regents of the University of California v. Bakke* rules that there is a constitutionally compelling interest in allowing state universities to factor race into their admission decisions to achieve the benefits of diversity or as remedy for past discrimination.
1979	Johnson becomes acting dispatcher.
1979	The Supreme Court's 5-to-2 decision in *United Steelworkers of America v. Weber* (1979) rules that Title VII does not prohibit race-conscious affirmative action plans, if those plans are temporary and goal- rather than quota-oriented.
1980	Johnson and Joyce apply for dispatcher's job. Both are among seven finalists. Johnson scores better on exam, but Joyce is given the job on recommendation of the agency's affirmative action officer.

1980–1982	Joyce works as agency's dispatcher.
January 1981	Ronald Reagan inaugurated as nation's fortieth president. His Supreme Court and Justice Department appointments initiate the decline of federal support for affirmative action programs.
March 1981	James Dawson, Johnson's attorney, lodges complaint with Equal Employment Opportunity Commission and decides to sue in federal court.
May 1982	Trial opens Friday in Ninth Federal Circuit Court presided over by Judge William A. Ingram.
August 1982	Judge Ingram decides in favor of Johnson, arguing that the county's affirmative action did not measure up to criteria established in Title VII and *Weber* and thus was discriminatory.
Spring 1983	Agency gives Johnson dispatcher's job, reassigns Joyce to another dispatcher position in a different yard.
February 1984	Ingram's decision reviewed by three-judge panel in Ninth Circuit Court of Appeals.
December 1984	Ninth Circuit Court of Appeals reverses district court's decision, arguing that Judge Ingram had interpreted Title VII and *Weber* too narrowly.
December 1984	Johnson decides to retire.
September 1985	Ninth Circuit Court refuses to rehear arguments *en banc*.
December 1985	Constance Brooks, a public interest lawyer with Mountain States Legal Foundation, petitions for a writ of certiorari — i.e., appeals to the Supreme Court to hear Johnson's case.
February 1986	Supreme Court justices confer to consider Johnson's petition.
July 1986	Supreme Court agrees to review circuit court's decision during next term.
1986	Chief Justice Warren Burger retires. William Rehnquist becomes new chief justice. Antonin Scalia becomes the newest and most conservative member of the Court.
1986	In *Wygant v. Jackson Board of Education* the Supreme Court's 5-to-4 decision emphasizes that affirmative action plans must clearly establish pattern of "prior discrimination."

November 1986	The Supreme Court convenes to hear Johnson's case on November 12. On November 14 the justices confer and in a 6-to-3 vote uphold the Ninth Circuit Court's reversal of the district court's decision.
March 1987	Supreme Court announces its decision in *Johnson v. Santa Clara.*
1988	*Bakke* author Lewis Powell retires and is replaced by Anthony Kennedy, after Robert Bork's controversial nomination fails.
July 1995	Board of Regents of University of California ends its affirmative action program.
March 1996	The Fifth Circuit Court of Appeals in *Hopwood v. State of Texas* invalidates the use of racial preferences in admitting candidates to the state's colleges and thus repudiates *Bakke.*
July 1996	The Supreme Court refuses to hear the State of Texas' appeal and lets stand the appellate court's ruling.
November 1996	California passes the Civil Rights Initiative, barring colleges within the state from using racial or gender preferences in admissions, hiring, and contracting.

INDEX